The
POWER
to
PREVAIL

The
POWER
to
PREVAIL

Turning Your Adversities into Advantages

DAVID FOSTER

WARNER
Faith™

A Division of AOL Time Warner Book Group

"Hero" © 1993 Sony/ATV Songs LLC, Stay Straight Music, Hidden Pun Music. All rights on behalf of Sony/ATV Songs LLC & Stay Straight Music administered by Sony/ATV Music Pub., 8 Music Square West, Nashville, TN 37203. All rights reserved. Used by permission.

Scripture quotations noted KJV are from the KING JAMES VERSION of the Holy Bible.

Scripture quotations noted nlt are from the Holy Bible, New Living Translation, copyright © 1996. Used by permission of Tyndale House Publishers, Inc., Wheaton, Illinois 60189. All rights reserved.

Scripture quotations noted THE MESSAGE are from *The Message: The New Testament in Contemporary English.* Copyright © 1993 by Eugene H. Peterson.

Scripture quotations noted NIV are from the HOLY BIBLE: NEW INTERNATIONAL VERSION®. Copyright © 1973, 1978, 1984 by International Bible Society. Used by permission of Zondervan Publishing House. All rights reserved.

Scripture quotations noted TLB are from *The Living Bible,* copyright © 1971. Used by permission of Tyndale House Publishers, Inc., Wheaton, Illinois 60189. All rights reserved.

Scripture quotations noted NRSV are from the NEW REVISED STANDARD VERSION of the Bible. Copyright © 1989 by the Division of Christian Education of the National Council of The Churches of Christ in the U.S.A. All rights reserved.

Warner Books, Inc., 1271 Avenue of the Americas,
New York, NY 10020

Visit our Web site at www.twbookmark.com.

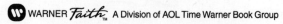 WARNER *Faith* A Division of AOL Time Warner Book Group

Printed in the United States of America

First Printing: August 2003

10 9 8 7 6 5 4 3 2 1

The Library of Congress Cataloging-in-Publication Data
Foster, David
    The power to prevail : turning your adversities into advantages / David Foster.
    p. cm.
    Includes bibliographical references.
    ISBN 0-446-53120-0
    1. Suffering—Religious aspects—Christianity. 2. Success—Religious aspects—Christianity. I. Title

BV4909.F67 2003

238.8'6—dc21   2003043268

Contents

⌣

Adversity Is Not Optional

The good things which belong to prosperity are to be wished, but the good things that belong to adversity are to be admired.

—SENECA

Life is hard. It is hard by the yard, by the inch, by the day, by the hour, and sometimes by the minute. It shouldn't be, but it is.

God's ideal was a paradise called Eden. Into this lush, idyllic, and perfect world, he planted our parents, Adam and Eve. He gave them the one power that separated them from all of God's creation: the power to choose. And the choices they made then continue to make trouble for us now. When they chose to have it their own way by disobeying God, they turned their advantages into adversities. Since that time, adversity has not been optional for anyone in any age.

DREAMING OF THE PERFECT WORLD

Since none of us like adversity, we dream of a time and place where life could be ordered up like the perfect meal. What would you choose if someone handed you a "Preferred Life Menu," on which you could find everything needed for the perfect life?

Maybe you would start out with the basics: happiness, health, and enough money to enjoy both and worry about neither. You would certainly want good friends and a family that loves you. No doubt, you would want meaningful work for which you got handsomely paid, along with a reputation for staggering success, yet without sacrificing plenty of free time for rest and recreation. If you are the daring type, you might order a dessert of real-life adventures able to take you to exotic locations where you could accomplish amazing feats of bravery. And for after-dinner entertainment, you might want to hang out with the rich and famous.

I'm reasonably confident that you would choose some or all of these things. But the one thing I'm betting you would *not* choose would be a heaping helping of hard times. Who in his or her right mind goes out looking for trouble? The answer is, no one does—and they don't have to. In the real world, trouble comes looking for you. Life has a way of getting hard overnight as well as over time and without warning. The world you sit on top of one day can roll over on you the next. Still, we dream of that risk-free, safe world. We sail on in our search for a secure harbor and friendly waters.

Our natural aversion to adversity, along with a strong desire for adventure, may help to explain why we have built the most safety-conscious culture of all time. In our zeal to avoid risk we have ended up settling for "Life Lite"—a slice of the zest and excitement we've always wanted, but with none of the bitter taste of adversity that goes hand in hand with an adventurous soul living in a dangerous world.

Early life lessons on how to ride a two-wheel bike felt as natural to me as chewing gum and walking at the same time. Not once did I consider, nor did my parents insist, that I wear a nerdy-looking safety helmet. I knew that occasionally I would fall off my bike and that I should try to avoid failing headfirst. I fully realized that life and danger go hand in hand and I respected that—but I didn't know enough to feel paralyzed by it. I merely accepted that falling is a part of living, as is getting back up after the fall.

But things have changed in our safety-obsessed society. Today, loving parents wouldn't think of letting their children ride a bike or a skateboard without a helmet, elbow pads, kneepads, mirrors on the handlebars, reflective tape on the fenders, and a bell in an easy-to-reach position. And just in case a few daredevil parents might still be running around out there, our guardian, the government, mandates that the nation's children wear helmets.

We have become protection-conscious and alarmed to the teeth. Safety devices that warn, scream, scare, and call for help hang from our belts, get wired into our cars and computers, and built into our homes. And while I, too, avoid adversity whenever possible, I can't help but wonder if we haven't traded the joy and adventure that are life itself for the uneasy comfort of easily circumvented and often-broken high-tech safety devices. Don't get me wrong. I am for safety—but do we really want a fail-safe world, or a safe-to-fail world?

WHAT BIBLE ARE WE READING?

Even religion has gotten into the act. People flock to hear fair-weather sermons delivered by power-suited preachers who promise the good life with God. In an attempt to attract men and women back to God and make Jesus more appealing, every Sunday of the year fast-moving discourses focus more on our happiness than our holiness.

Parishioners get fed a steady diet of faith formulas and religious moralisms. They receive superficial steps on how to be more like Moses, be more like David, be bold and fearless like John the Baptist, be aggressive like Peter or strategic like Paul, or just be more like Jesus in every way—and life, they hear, will become easier, healthier, happier, and, most important of all, more prosperous.

And I wonder, *What Bible are these people reading?*

Moses lived in desert exile for more than forty years. David committed adultery and had to flee from his own son, who wanted him dead. John the Baptist lost his head to an executioner's sword. Peter died on a cross. Paul got locked in prison until the Romans finally killed him. Jesus suffered betrayal, beatings, and crucifixion. *No one* who walked with God by faith failed to slog through long, hellish periods of adversity, ranging from the loss of basic creature comforts to running for their very lives.

Adversity is not optional, *especially* with God!

Jesus himself said, "In this world you will have tribulation." He insisted that we can expect doses of not just trouble, but tribulation. Tribulation is trouble on steroids—but that's only where it begins. In the same breath Jesus also said, "Be of good cheer; I have overcome the world" (John 16:33 KJV). He meant that a real-life encounter with the ultimate Overcomer is no mere life-enhancing option, but a soul-saving, trouble-transforming necessity.

So if that's the case, then where are the clarion voices extolling the virtues of the overcoming power (not the go-around power) of the resurrected Christ? Today we hear about six quick ways to fix what's wrong, or seven simple steps to cope with stress, or ten towering techniques for getting what we want *now*. But simplistic solutions can never yield an effortless victory. At best they produce disillusioned listeners who blame themselves; at worst, they blame God.

Too many of us long for a time and place that is neither hot nor cold. We like it mild. We don't like it black or white because we've gotten so used to beige. We don't like to sweat; that's why we created deodorant. Why would God allow someone to invent the umbrella and the elevator if he wanted us to walk in the rain or up the stairs? Today we have cars with CD players, video and stereo systems so that we can have all the comforts of home on the road. Some cars even have onboard GPS computers that do everything from giving directions to a favorite restaurant to unlocking car doors for forgetful drivers who left keys in the ignition.

And what has happened to us in this safety-obsessed, easy-fix, pleasure-seeking world of ours? We have become people with lives a mile wide and an inch thick. Like brittle ice, however, the least amount of pressure cracks up the whole thing. *We* are cracking up . . . and many of us feel content to stay that way.

Yet denying the certainty of adversity serves only to make us weaker, not stronger. Even if we could hermetically seal ourselves away from sickness and sorrow, we would be short-circuiting the very events, people, and places that God wants to use to mold us and make us into the amazing people we so desperately long to be. Those whom God uses mightily, he first wounds deeply.

I have watched this principle at work in my own life and in the lives of countless thousands. I have seen individuals respond to adversity with amazing courage and stamina. I have watched men and women bury their dreams, their businesses, their careers, and even their children, and yet come out of those dark experiences with more faith and more determination than ever. At the same time, I have seen others go through things that don't seem to be all that hard and strange, yet their experiences crush them. Rather than becoming better and stronger, they grow bitter and weaker. I have learned that adversity, by itself, makes no one stronger; only a proper response to adversity has the power to bring us astonishing strength.

This book seeks to shine a light into the shadows of adversity. And not just a small, faint, flickering candlelight, but a bright, bold, burning floodlight of hope from the teaching of Christ and the application of his timeless truth to our everyday experiences. Everything in this book flows from a basic premise:

> Adversity is not an option; it is a fact of life. The fact of adversity is not our real problem, but rather the attitudes we adopt and the choices we make in the face of it. Those choices and attitudes separate those who prevail from those who don't.

Adversity can be our ally. We grow strong not in spite of our adversities, but because of them. We need not fear them, only face them. God has given us the power to take control of our lives, even though he alone retains the right to control the conditions and circumstances under which we live. He means for fear, uncertainty, and doubt to drive us to him. We have no "Sunday school" God who lives only in the Bible, but a real God who wants to help us as we face adversity in the real world. Through faith we can turn our lives around the moment we choose a different perspective.

Joseph displayed this very attitude in the face of his brothers' betrayal. Even after they sold him into slavery, he told them, "You intended to harm me, but God intended it for good" (Gen. 50:20 NIV).

Have you ever stopped to think that your weaknesses and handicaps may actually be the key to your usefulness to God and to the world?

The key to prevailing in the face of adversity lies in your power to choose. God gave you the power to choose your attitude (the way you feel), your aptitude (the way you think), and your actions (your daily habits). Don't let anyone with a suit and a smile sell you a formula for a pain-free, stain-free, strain-free life. The power to prevail lies in your knowing and mastering these three powerful response-abilities. It is to that pursuit that we now turn our attention.

The
POWER
to
PREVAIL

1

Turning Crawling into Climbing

Do not follow where the path may lead.
Go instead where there is no path and leave a trail.

—MURIEL STRODE

At the top of my "all-time best memories" list stands the moment I brought my firstborn home from the hospital. I carried Erin around the house while spewing baby talk to try to make her smile. I cherish the memory of rocking her to sleep!

But as much as I loved carrying her, she quickly tired of it. As she grew stronger and bolder she wanted to crawl. Crawling quickly turned into pulling up on a chair leg, and pulling up turned into climbing. She started by climbing up and down the stairs, followed soon after by climbing up and down the furniture in the house, the car in the garage, and the trees in the yard. She climbed as if she had an internal climbing gear. My wife called me home one day because our sweet, precious, dainty baby girl had climbed up a chest of drawers so high that the thing toppled over.

For her own good and our peace of mind, we forbade her to climb. She climbed anyway. We threatened to punish her. Her climbing continued. One day I brought home a little trike called an "Olle," a yellow plastic thing with four wheels low to the ground. I hoped she might take to coasting along on her Olle, but this proved only a momentary distraction from her real passion, climbing.

In the end we could come up with only one safe solution. We put in a swing set so she could at least have a safe place to climb. She loved it. It gave her many more creative ways to climb. She found ways to hang off the high bar by her hands and feet, ways that sometimes took my breath away. I took comfort in the thought that maybe, as the firstborn, she just felt bored. But when little sisters one and two arrived, they *all* climbed! My wife and I faithfully delivered our warnings, but our daughters heedlessly continued their fanatical climbing.

I have since concluded that all kids are born with an internal climbing gear. Could it be that we humans will always feel dissatisfied with crawling or coasting so long as we have something close by to climb?

TWO OF GOD'S BEST GIFTS

My daughters taught me what I have since then seen reinforced: God created us to climb. He has given each of us a climbing gear and an ascending spirit.

To a child, climbing seems as natural as breathing. Despite our anxieties, we adults tend to accept that reality. But if we see climbing as merely a childish habit to overcome, we may miss the genius of our wiring.

In my younger days, the adults in my life urged me to trade in childish things to become a man. People even quoted the Bible to prove their point. Innumerable times I've heard the apostle Paul's instruction: "When I was a child, I talked like a child, I thought like a child, I reasoned like a child. When I became a man, I put childish ways behind me" (1 Cor. 13:11 NIV). Well-meaning folks used this verse to "prove" that nothing of childhood should be taken into adulthood. But over time I've come to understand that Paul never intended for us to jettison the best of what it means to be a born climber.

God gave us a climbing gear and an ascending spirit in order to prepare us to prevail over adversity. He dropped us into this competitive, sometimes dark, always dangerous world equipped to live as victors, not victims. We find the difference between those who turn adversity into an advantage and those who don't, not in their abilities, but in their response-abilities.

An old saying goes, "Don't make a mountain out of a molehill." While I agree with that philosophy, I think the greater danger is that, in the face of adversity, we will settle for staring at a molehill and miss the mountain altogether. But you and I will *never* feel satisfied with playing in the mud when the summit calls us onward and upward.

Within each human heart beats an incredibly strong drive to prevail. To meet that need we must learn to use our two best gifts: our climbing gear and our ascending spirit. We will never feel satisfied to settle for less than standing, triumphantly, on the summit of a hill worth climbing. Too many submarine their more noble callings for less honorable urges. But why coast or crawl over the molehill of least resistance, when you know your God-given birthright calls you to experience the thrill of standing atop a mountain worth climbing? Why not look out at life from the summit of a great peak rather than up from a mud hole? The ancient Roman poet Propertius said it this way: "Great is the road I climb, but the garland offered by an easier effort is not worth the gathering." In the real world, easy doesn't do it.

FACING LIFE AS IT IS

Healthy individuals strive to discover and define the reality around them. We classify people who refuse to face real life as either psychotic or neurotic.

When you ask a psychotic person, "What is two plus two?" he will answer "five," "seven," or "ten," because he has lost touch with reality. On the other hand, if you ask a neurotic, "What is two plus two?" she can give you the right answer—"four"—but she fusses, "Why does it have to be four? Why can't it be something else?" While psychotics live in a fantasyland of their own making, neurotics see the world as it is and freeze in the face of its hard, sometimes harsh realities. They feel "harassed and helpless," in Jesus' words (Matt. 9:36 NIV). Their ragged nerves keep their hair-trigger tempers barely under control. As Alvin Toffler puts it, "Millions of people are terminally fed up." Such individuals normally slip into lifestyle patterns of either crawling or coasting.

CLIMBERS SEE LIFE DIFFERENTLY

Everyone wants to prevail in life, but not everyone does. I've often asked, "What makes the difference? Why do some people prevail in the midst of adversity while others fold and fail?" The answer usually comes in the choices they make.

Climbers accept that while they cannot control what happens to them, they can control "what happens" to what happens to them. They take control of their lives by taking control of their choices.

On the other hand, crawlers and coasters—even exceptional men and women with all the advantages of success—lack this basic will to choose. In the face of dead ends, detours, or dry holes, they revert to childish habits. Why? Maybe they enjoyed so many advantages along the way that they think they deserve a strain-free, stain-free, pain-free future. Perhaps others have pushed and pulled them along for so long that they get angry and downright indignant every time they face anything bigger than a molehill.

But while anyone can coast right over a molehill, no one coasts up a mountain, any more than they can drift upstream. Coasters cry out for a level (or slightly tilted in their favor) playing field, or else they quit. If they can't coast, they refuse to climb. But cry as they will and complain as they might, life just will not tilt to their favor. Both crawlers and coasters waste their lives looking for favorable winds and perfect circumstances. But as George Bernard Shaw said, "The people who get on in this world are the people who get up and look for the circumstances they want, and, if they can't find them, make them."

When you ask mountain climbers why they risk their health, their fortunes, and even their lives to climb a mountain, many answer with the classic "Because it's there." But climbers in the real human race have more substantial reasons for their efforts. It was Pascal, the seventeenth-century French philosopher and mathematician, who said, "The heart has its reasons which reason knows nothing of." He recognized that God created the heart to be the human control center. No matter how big my brain or strong my hand, my heart controls them both. And if my control center gets damaged or depleted, the rest of my body suffers and eventually atrophies.

Climbers prevail because they never lose heart. When pushed, they push back—not with their hand, but with their heart. They refuse to relent, retreat, or resign themselves to the way things are. They don't lean on their emotions, because they know emotions are fickle and unpredictable. Developing their heart muscle gives them the ability to respond to the changing conditions of the climb. Sooner than later they acknowledge that things are what they are. If they face a steep mountain in threatening or bleak conditions, they simply acknowledge the reality and climb on.

In contrast, crawlers and coasters live out of their emotions. They see adversity as an unfair hardship. They play the victim. Their fluctuating emotions thrive on innuendo and false perceptions. They feel sure that the mountain is impassable and its conditions are unbearable, not because they have ever visited the mountain, but because they listen to others who stopped climbing a long time ago. Crawlers look for someone to blame for the way things are. Stuart Briscoe noted that "discouragement comes when you try to start with what you wish you had but don't have. And it intensifies when you insist on trying to be in a position you are not in and probably never will be in."[1]

By contrast, climbers accept reality, adjust their attitude, and align their energies to begin taking action based on what is—all without losing heart or drowning in self-pity. They don't waste their time blaming God, defaming others, or shaming themselves.

Climbers See Life as a Gift to Be Exploited

Solomon reminds us, "When God gives any man wealth and possessions, and enables him to enjoy them, to accept his lot and be happy in his work—this is a gift of God" (Eccl. 5:19 NIV).

When my children were very young, they seemed as likely to play with the boxes that held their Christmas presents as with the gifts themselves. But as they matured, they tore through the wrapping and ripped open the boxes to get to the treasures inside. And I welcomed the change. I would have felt hurt if, after going to all the trouble and expense to buy them what they said they wanted, they either didn't play with the gift or failed to show gratitude.

How, then, must God feel when we take this great gift called life and refuse to unwrap it and enjoy it?

In the 1989 motion picture *Dead Poets Society,* Robin Williams plays a teacher in an exclusive eastern prep school. On the first day of school, he takes his class of boys into the hallway to look at pictures of deceased graduates. He motivates them to excel in life with the following words: "We are food for worms, lads! Believe it or not, each and every one of us in this room one day will stop breathing, turn cold, and die. Step forward and see these faces from the past. They were just like you are now. They believe they're destined for great things. Their eyes are full of hope. But, you see, gentlemen, these boys are now fertilizing daffodils. If you listen real close, you will hear them whisper their legacy to you. Lean in. What do you hear?" Then Robin says in an eerie voice, *"Carpe Diem!"* (Latin for "seize the day"). "Seize the day, boys! Make your lives extraordinary!"

Such is the climbers' mantra: seize the day and climb on!

Today is God's gift to you. What you do with it is your gift to God and to the world around you. This very moment, as you read these words, as your heart beats, and as you contemplate why you live at this moment in history, don't forget to enjoy your own private miracle of life. Don't allow adversity to bankrupt your today by paying interest on the regrets of yesterday and borrowing in advance against the troubles of tomorrow. Plan on purpose to live fully and well now.

Today is the day to begin turning your adversities into your advantages. Right now is the best time to decide to enjoy this matchless gift of God called "my life." Remember, yesterday is a canceled check, and tomorrow is a promissory note; but today is cash in your hands, which must be invested or lost forever. As William James said so well, "Where is it, this present? It has melted in our grasp, fled ere we could touch it, gone in the instant of becoming."

Now is the time to place your trust and confidence, as well as your doubts and fears, into God's hands. You will never regret trusting a good God who wants more for you than you've ever dared to want for yourself. The moment you see life as a gift from God and trust his plan for your life, things begin to change. The Bible makes this promise: "For God did not give us a spirit of timidity, but a spirit of power, of love and of self-discipline" (2 Tim. 1:7 NIV). Boldly and bravely tear open this gift called life and use it up to its fullest.

Climbers See Life as an Abundance to Be Explored

Climbers have an abundance mentality; crawlers and coasters cling to a scarcity mentality. Climbers look at life through the lens of faith, while others allow fear to make them nearsighted. To see the difference, I invite you to get to know one of my favorite characters in the Bible: Caleb.

As a young man, Caleb and another climber named Joshua received orders to spy out the Promised Land (along with ten other men who proved to be crawlers and coasters). Moses directed them to do a careful cost-benefit analysis for occupying the new territory. He told them to "see what the land is like and whether the people who live there are strong or weak, few or many" (Num. 13:18 NIV). Twelve men went out and twelve men returned . . . with two very different reports.

Everyone agreed that the land was indeed everything God had promised it would be. "We went into the land to which you sent us," they said, "and it does flow with milk and honey!" (Num. 13:27 NIV). But the majority struck fear into the hearts of the people by telling them that the inhabitants looked too big, too strong, too many, and their cities too fortified, for the Israelites ever to hope for victory. They saw only what their coasters' and crawlers' mind-set would allow them to see: problems and impossibilities.

Joshua and Caleb presented the minority report. They, too, saw the abundance of the land and the formidable inhabitants and their well-defended cities. But because they could see with their hearts, not just their heads, they came to vastly different conclusions. Caleb had the courage to step straight into this circus of chaos that the negative report had created and dared pose another possibility: "We should go up and take possession of the land, for we can certainly do it" (Num. 13:30 NIV). He knew how hard it would be to go forward, but he had no intention of retreating into the desert. Caleb knew then what we know now—anything worth having requires a fight. He revealed his faith and fighting spirit when he said, "Only do not rebel against the LORD. And do not be afraid of the people of the land, because we will swallow them up. Their protection is gone, but the LORD is with us. Do not be afraid of them" (Num. 14:9 NIV).

Have you ever noticed that it takes only one negative person to ruin a meeting or gathering? Everything can be going smoothly, but let one negative voice arise from within the group, and everyone feels paralyzed. That's when we need climbers more than ever. When the crawlers see God only through the lens of adversity, we need climbers who see adversity only through the lens of God.

When God spoke to Moses after the ten crawlers had delivered their message, he said, "How long will these people treat me with contempt? How long will they refuse to believe in me, in spite of all the miraculous signs I have performed among them?" (Num. 14:11 NIV). Although God vowed that every one of those who bought into the crawlers' report would die crawling around the desert, he promised, "Because my servant Caleb has a different spirit and follows me wholeheartedly, I will bring him into the land he went to, and his descendants will inherit it" (Num. 14:24 NIV). Notice that it was a different *spirit,* not a different mind or a better plan, that drove Caleb to believe that what God promised, God could and would provide. He wholeheartedly believed that God would make a way, despite the difficulties. He considered the Promised Land a mountain worth scaling, no matter the threat.

Like Caleb, climbers see life as an abundance to be explored. Jesus said, "I came so they can have real and eternal life, more and better life than they ever dreamed of" (John 10:10 THE MESSAGE). The climbers' abundance mentality can't be measured, quantified, or traded on the commodities market. It is not just more of the same old stuff that never has satisfied us and never will.

We Americans tend to see abundance through a success paradigm. For us, success means more. Consider the story of an American tourist who docked his boat in a tiny Mexican village. Impressed by the quality of the fish, he asked a fisherman how long it took him to make his catch.

"Not very long," answered the Mexican.

"Why not stay out longer and catch more?" asked the American. The fisherman explained that he already had caught all he needed.

"But what do you do with the rest of your time?" asked the American.

"I sleep late, play with my children, take a siesta with my wife, and in the evenings I go into the village to see my friends, drink coffee, play the guitar, and sing a few songs."

The American could hardly contain himself. "You'll never be successful that way," he protested. "You should start fishing longer every day. You can then sell the extra fish you catch. With the revenue, you can buy a bigger boat. With the extra money the larger boat will bring, you can buy a second one and a third one and so on until you have an entire fleet of trawlers. Instead of selling your fish to a middleman, you can negotiate directly with the processing plants and maybe even open your own plant. You can then leave this little village and move to Mexico City, Los Angeles, or even New York City! From there you can direct your huge enterprise."

"And how long would that take?" asked the fisherman.

"Twenty, maybe twenty-five years," replied the American. "And after your business gets really big, you can start selling stocks and make millions!"

"Millions?"

"Yes, millions. And after that, you'll be able to retire, live in a tiny village near the coast, sleep late, play with your grandchildren, catch a few fish, take a siesta with your wife, and spend your evenings drinking coffee and playing the guitar with your friends!"

Some people call this abundant living, but actually it is just another form of climbing the wrong hill. Jesus put it this way: "Beware! Don't always be wishing for what you don't have. For real life and real living are not related to how rich we are" (Luke 12:15 TLB). In his breakthrough research on adversity and achievement, Paul Stoltz said it this way: "Success can be defined as the degree to which one moves forward and upward, progressing in one's lifelong mission, despite all obstacles or other forms of adversity."[2] Success does not mean more so much as it means climbing higher on the trek toward the summit of God's true abundance.

Climbers See Life as an Adventure to Be Enjoyed

Climbers live with an undiminished and unabated capacity for curiosity. They see life as an adventure to be enjoyed, not as a long series of indignities to be endured. As Søren Kierkegaard, the nineteenth-century Danish philosopher, put it, "If I were to wish for anything, I should not wish for wealth and power, but for the passionate sense of the potential, for the eye which, ever young and ardent, sees the possible."

Climbers waste no time riding or beating dead horses. They opt for the thrill of taming and riding bucking broncos.

Climbers See Life as a Mountain to Be Conquered

Let's return to our fellow climber Caleb and fast-forward in his life forty-five years. He is now eighty-five. He has outlived all his peers except Joshua. He has earned the right to take it easy—but Caleb is a true climber. He sees life as a mountain to be conquered.

Surely Caleb has had enough excitement for two lifetimes! He has seen Egyptian bonds break, the Red Sea part, water flow from a rock, manna fall from heaven, and the death of all his friends, other than Joshua, as they dropped one-by-one through unbelief. A climber at heart, Caleb has both witnessed and participated in the nation's triumphal entry into the Promised Land. And now, at age eighty-five, he is one of the first to choose where he wants to live out the rest of his life. And what would a climber choose? Another mountain, of course! He told Joshua,

> *I am still as strong today as the day Moses sent me out; I'm just as vigorous to go out to battle now as I was then. Now give me this hill country that the LORD promised me that day. You yourself heard then that the Anakites were there and their cities were large and fortified, but, the LORD helping me, I will drive them out just as he said.*
> (Josh. 14:11–12 NIV)

Here was an old man who had outlived all his peers—and he requested only one last mountain to climb. Caleb knew that we all need something worth doing to give our life meaning.

Like Caleb, I want to be a life-changing, soul-feeding, spirit-lifting force during my brief time here. I want to shape my world, not merely be shaped by it. Daily I pray, "Lord, wake me up before I die," not "If I should die before I wake . . ." Climbers refuse to spend their lives being normal or doing business as usual. They strain and strive for the chance to change the world for good, for God, and forever.

It was Ovid, the first-century poet, who said, "Happy is he who dares courageously to defend what he loves."

Many important events in the Bible took place on or near mountains. God called Moses to lead his people out of bondage on Mount Horeb. After the Exodus, God commanded Moses to gather the people at Mount Sinai to receive the Ten Commandments. Moses died and was buried on Mount Nebo. Elijah, one of Israel's greatest prophets, defeated the prophets of Baal on Mount Carmel.

Much of the life and ministry of Jesus took place on mountains. Satan tempted him on a mountain (Matt. 4:8). We call Jesus' most famous teaching session "the Sermon on the Mount" (Matt. 5–7). Jesus repeatedly went up a mountain to pray (Luke 6:12). He enjoyed his transfiguration on a mountain (Matt. 17:1–8). And at the end, his enemies crucified him at a place called Mount Calvary.

The Bible also uses the term "mountain" as a symbol of stability (Ps. 30:7). Mountains represent places where God shows his power (Ps. 121:1–2), sometimes through their flattening. In Isaiah 40:4 God promises, "Every mountain and hill [shall be] made low."

If you're a climber, you need an appropriate mountain to climb. You won't feel satisfied with anything less. Psychologist Abraham Maslow discovered the same truth when he said, "If you deliberately plan to be less than you are capable of being, then I warn you that you'll be unhappy for the rest of your life."

THREE THINGS ALL CLIMBERS NEED

Climbers never revert to crawling and coasting just because life gets hard. You'll never hear a climber sit around and whine about how unfair life is or how bad she has it. Climbers are champions at heart. They are winners, not whiners. They respond to life, not react to it. And all of them have at least three things in common.

All Climbers Need a Climber's Perspective

Climbers know that life can get hard and dangerous without a moment's notice. Things seldom go as planned. But climbers have this perspective: if God still reigns in heaven, and his love still flows toward them, and they remain in his care, they need only to climb on.

Climbers think differently from others. They know that at their center, at the core of their being, rings out the call to ascend. And how do you know whether you have a climber's perspective? Suppose I were to ask a writer why he writes. I will get one of three answers. If he has a crawler's perspective, he will say, "I write for recognition." If he has a coaster's perspective, he will say, "I write for the money." If he has a climber's perspective, he will say, "I write because I must."

A climber climbs because that's what he *is*. To be who he is, he must do what he does—climb. If you labor only for recognition, there will never be recognition enough. If you live for money, there will never be money enough. But if you write or paint or build or teach or any other of a thousand things because you must in order to be who God made you to be, then you have discovered the secret of living for an audience of one. And climbing for his pleasure is enough.

The climber's perspective can be summed up in two words: "Climb on." While climbers accept that they seldom control their environment or their circumstances, they exercise the power to choose their attitude and reactions to what happens to them and so climb on. Climbers climb in the cold and they climb in the heat. They climb when it's steep and even when there seems to be no way. Why? Because they know that climbing is what God created them to do. *And if God wants me to climb,* they think, *he will make a way.* So they climb on!

Fellow climber, climb on when you seem to be climbing alone. Climb on when you can't see your way ahead. Climb on when all you see behind are gullies and ditches and all you see ahead are cliffs and threatening overhangs. Climb on, though the path seems uncertain. Climb on, knowing that just around the next turn God may be waiting with a breakthrough. Climb on, because life is too precious to waste on coasting or crawling.

Stand up on your two good feet, face the summit, and ascend with the conviction that the one who loved you enough to place you on that mountain, loves you still. He promises you the power to climb: "I can do everything through him who gives me strength" (Phil. 4:13 NIV). He pledges to protect you while you climb: "I lift up my eyes to the hills— where does my help come from? My help comes from the LORD, the Maker of heaven and earth. He will not let your foot slip—he who watches over you will not slumber" (Ps. 121:1–3 NIV). And he guarantees you that on your climb, "no temptation has seized you except what is common to man. And God is faithful; he will not let you be tempted beyond what you can bear. But when you are tempted, he will also provide a way out so that you can stand up under it" (1 Cor. 10:13 NIV).

Climb on!

Climbers Need the Right Mountains

You won't find a climber sniffing around a molehill or playing in a mud hole. Climbers recognize that the difference between molehills and mountains comes not in their degree of difficulty, but in their significance.

Climbers don't look for easy going, but they must know that their efforts are worth the sacrifice. As fully alive human beings, they understand that life is not about getting more and bigger stuff. Climbers have the ability to admire without the need to acquire. They look for something way beyond success. They want significance.

The wildly successful 1987 album *Joshua Tree,* by the Irish supergroup U2, features a single titled, "I Still Haven't Found What I'm Looking For." The song cries out for significance. One of its lines says, "I have climbed the highest mountains, I have run through the fields, . . . but I still haven't found what I'm looking for."

This could be the cry of our generation.

When I climb, I want a mountain that's significant. And how do I recognize significance? For one, getting to the summit will make a difference in the lives of others. I don't want to struggle up a mountain that shows no promise of positively impacting men and women. Climbers know that the "more stuff" mountain, or the "bigger car" mountain, or the "nicer house" mountain, or even the "corner office" mountain, just isn't worth a big chunk of their lives. They refuse to fight their way to the summit of a mountain unworthy of the climb.

Naturally, climbers get discouraged like everyone else. They get tired, bruised, bored, and, at times, they break down. How do they keep going? By remembering that they are climbing toward a summit that, once reached, will make all the pain and sacrifice well worth the effort.

Remember this: if it doesn't love something, lift something, build something, appreciate something, and bring God pleasure, it is nothing but a molehill, a heap of mud, or a pile of manure. On the other hand, mountains worth climbing are made of pure gold.

Climbers Need the Right Climbing Companions

In his best-selling book *Good to Great,* Jim Collins claims that it's more important to have the right people in your life or organization than to have a compelling vision and direction.

> The good to great leaders understood three simple truths. First, if you begin with "who," rather than "what," you can more easily adapt to a changing world. If people join the bus primarily because of where it is going, what happens if you get ten miles down the road and you need to change direction? You've got a problem. But if people are on the bus because of who else is on the bus, then it's much easier to change direction: "Hey, I got on this bus because of who else is on it; if we need to change direction to be more successful, fine with me."
>
> Second, if you have the right people on the bus, the problem of how to motivate and manage people largely goes away. The right people don't need to be tightly managed or fired up; they will be self-motivated by the inner drive to produce the best results and to be part of creating something great.
>
> Third, if you have the wrong people, it doesn't matter whether you discover the right direction; you *still* won't have great company. Great vision without great people is irrelevant.[3]

I want climbing companions. Do you know what climbing companions do? They encourage you at the right moment. They do exactly what you need, when you need it. And they're careful not to criticize you brutally, because they're on the same climb. They know it's hard.

As a climber, I need the right people on "my bus." The biblical axiom "Do not be misled: 'Bad company corrupts good character'" (1 Cor. 15:33 NIV) remains true. You will mirror the behavior of the dominant personalities around you. If you hang around a bunch of negative, whining people, you will become a negative, whining person. But if you stick close to faith-filled, hope-filled climbers, you'll also become faith-filled and hope-filled.

CREATED FOR ADVANCE

You are a natural-born climber. And all climbers know that adversity is not a choice.

Your lifetime will present you with plenty of excuses to settle for crawling and coasting, but God has given you two very special gifts. You have a climbing gear in your heart, and a desire for high and noble achievement in your spirit. You were not created for retreat, but advance. You have the power to prevail against all odds as you learn to turn your adversities into advantages by using your God-given power of choice. You are a powerful person, and with God's help, you can build something beautiful out of the ashes of any adversity.

Climbers know that character develops, not in the calm of base camp, but in the howling winds of adversity. Under normal conditions, you might be good, but you'll never be great. Good times and pleasant conditions do not demand that you draw from the deep well of virtue and character. Character gives the power to choose a virtuous course of action under adverse circumstances—and that power to choose the right path under fire represents the highest form of human control.

Sure, you'll encounter many opportunities to quit and camp. When you go through hell, it's possible to stop and smell the smoke. In fact, you can become an expert on smoke and all its devastating effects. You can play the role of victim and blame circumstances, people, or even God. There are as many plausible reasons for fear and failure as there are people in the world and days in our lives. But that's not what you were made for—and deep down in your heart, you know it.

You can't escape the desire to climb something, conquer something, achieve something, win something, endure something, and in the end, plant your own victory flag on the summit of a life well spent. Life is too short and the stakes are too high for you to settle for constant excuse making and blame-placing.

The choice is yours, always yours alone. And that choice is your power. It cannot be handed off to someone else. It cannot be reserved for another day. *You* have the power to change your life. And that power begins by making a choice that leads to an attitude.

With the right attitude and God's help, you can learn to turn grief into gladness, fear into faith, can'ts into cans, jealousy into joy, regrets into resolve, and grief into gladness. Remember the immortal words of wisdom from Homer, the eighth-century B.C. Greek poet: "'Tis man's to fight, but heaven's to give success." And hear the words of Patricia Neal, an Oscar-winning actress, who observed while struggling to recover from a debilitating stroke, "A strong, positive mental attitude will create more miracles than any wonder drug."

Why do some people find a way to prevail and conquer, while others collapse? God gave you a very special gift at birth—a climbing gear. He gave it to you because you will need it. Jesus said, "I have told you these things, so that in me you may have peace. In this world you will have trouble. But take heart! I have overcome the world" (John 16:33 NIV).

Adversity is not optional. When it comes to you, as it most surely will, you can take comfort that at least you're not alone in your struggle. It is the fact of adversity and hardship that makes the invitation of Jesus so amazing: "Come unto me, all ye that labor and are heavy laden," he said, "and I will give you rest" (Matt. 11:28 KJV).

God stands ready to make sense of the senseless and return power to the powerless. And not only does he give us victory over our adversities, he uses them to make us stronger and better. God gave us a climbing gear and an ascending spirit so that we can reach the summit of our potential, that place toward which we journey all our lives.

2

_ᨆ_

Turning Grief
into Gladness

**The greatest discovery of my generation is that human beings can
alter their lives by altering their attitudes of mind.**

–WILLIAM JAMES

For most people, driving is about getting from one place to the next.
But for me, twenty dollars' worth of gas can be worth two thousand
dollars' worth of therapy.

Nearly all my "eureka moments" have come after a few hours of solitude behind the wheel. I find it amazing how the subconscious can
untie mental knots and smooth out emotional kinks during a cruise
away from the daily routine.

That's why I wanted to be alone on a recent road trip. My mother
requested that I drive up to inspect the new headstone she'd had placed
on my father's grave. I had neither the time nor inclination to make the
trip, but out of respect for her wishes and his memory, I drove two
hours north. Alone and with time to ponder the past, my mind turned
to my childhood and what seemed like simpler, saner days. Today it
seems like an idyllic time, the period before loss and grief diluted my
zest and zeal for life. How I long to be that naive and innocent again!

Like most county seats in Kentucky, my hometown revolved around the downtown square. Before the Super Wal-Marts of the world hit town, it served as the hub of commerce and remained a perpetual beehive of activity. Now it's just several rows of old buildings either standing empty or occupied by local and state government offices.

As I drove around the square, I saw the old Slinkers jewelry store, where I bought my wife's engagement ring. Today it stands abandoned. Next door is the old pool hall, where I spent more than my share of carefree afternoons. At the northeast end of the square I took a hard right, up West Washington Avenue. At one time, most of our small-town aristocracy lived on this street. I passed several big, white-on-white, southern-style homes and loads of freshly painted wrought iron. At the end of the road on the right stood the dilapidated railroad station; to the left, the entrance to our city cemetery. As I passed through the big, imposing iron gates, I felt a familiar sadness come over me. I suddenly remembered what I had been trying to forget for more than a year—my dad died too soon, with too much left unsaid between us.

I drove reluctantly to my dad's gravesite. The tombstone—a stately gray slab of granite—features on one side only the simple inscription of our family's name, in block letters. On the other side is my father's full name, Wilton Edward Foster, along with the years of his birth and death. Nothing ornate or ostentatious about it.

My "eureka" moment came when I saw, etched into the stone between the two dates, a simple dash. And then it hit me: my father's entire life had been reduced to a dash. People passing by could read his name, when he was born, when he died, but nothing about his life. I wondered if I needed to stand there and say to passersby, "I'm part of his dash! He had me, fought in a world war, and did a lot of other things in his dash." Instead of feeling sad that my father had died, my soul flooded with gladness that he had lived. Because my father lived in his dash, I am alive in mine.

It also struck me that my father is not so much dead as done. He is done in his dash; but I am still working on mine. Yea, God! Right there in that cemetery, surrounded by the remains and reminders of death, I came fully alive. It occurred to me that even as I stood in the land of the dead, I was about to reenter the land of the living. *I'm going to leave here,* I thought, *but these people are staying.*

And in an instant a trip I'd dreaded became a breakthrough. Finally, I saw before me a clear choice. I could turn my grief into gladness by looking at this event differently. I could be more glad that I had had my father than mad that he was gone.[1] When someone asked Michael Jordan, the basketball legend, how he dealt with the tragic murder of his father, he said, "I am thankful that I had my father for the first thirty-six years of my life. I had him in the formative years. I had him when I really needed him."

Like Michael, I can be grateful or hateful. So can you.

LIFE IN THE DASH

As I left the cemetery that afternoon, I took some extra time to read a few of the nearby headstones. The old cemetery contains the remains of soldiers from both sides of the Civil War. One inscription caught my eye: Asa Lewis, a young Confederate solder killed the day after Christmas, 1862. He fell at the battle of Stones River in Murfreesboro, Tennessee. The inscription read, "He displayed more than ordinary gallantry."

When I returned home, I looked up the word *gallantry*. It describes a person of spirited and conspicuous bravery. And I thought, *I want that said of me.* When my children and grandchildren stand at my gravesite and consider my dash, I want them to be able to say of me, "In his dash he knew gain and loss, victory and defeat—but in spite of it all, he prevailed. He chose to live nobly. He determined to turn loss into gain, bitterness into blessing, and grief into gladness." That's what I want said of me, and I'd be willing to bet that's what you want, too.

But to have it, to earn it, to leave such a legacy behind, will require an understanding of what it takes to excel in the real world of opposing sides, situations, and seasons.

Life Is Lived Between Two Opposing Sides

Every living being senses the tension between what is and what ought to be. On the one hand there is life, as it ought to be; on the other hand is the way things really are.

From the cradle to the grave, we hear that we ought to be more, do more, have more, and give more. You may walk with a limp from false comparisons that important people in your life have made between what you are and what they think you should be. It starts with innocent comparisons between siblings, and then moves to the larger family.

As an adult, you learn to accept that life isn't always the way it should be. There is your career, the way it ought to be and the way it really is. There is your husband, as he ought to be and as he is. There's your wife, as she ought to be and as she is. That's just life in the dash, isn't it? You have been compared and measured since the day you were born—so much so, you may think of yourself as the sum total of ways in which you have measured up or fallen short.

People reminisce about "the good old days" when things were more as they ought to be. But did such a place ever exist? If so, I've never found it. All of us, from the day we are born till the day we die, live with the inequities between what we dreamed life would be and what life actually is. We want a world of fairness and justice, yet live a life less noble and thus less fulfilling.

Nevertheless, I still long for the land of my dreams, a place where good always wins over evil and everyone lives happily ever after. Pop singers David Crosby and Phil Collins wrote and released a song back in the '80s called "Hero." They sing of the antihero who slays the dragon with his sword, only to turn around and kill the maiden with his kiss! How can this be? One verse illustrates the paradox beautifully:

> The reason she loved him was the reason I loved him too, because he never wondered what was right or wrong. He just knew. He just knew. And we wonder, yes we wonder, how do you make sense of this when the hero kills the maiden with his kiss—with his kiss?

A fairy tale clearly draws the lines between good and evil; but in the real world, things get blurred. You discovered that on the first day all hell broke loose in your otherwise simple world. For some, it's the memory of not getting picked for a sandlot football game. For others, it's not being nominated for homecoming court, or not making the basketball team. For still others, it's getting slapped in the face with the sickening news that your dad has died from a massive heart attack, or whispers between your parents as they try to break the news that Mom has cancer, or worse still, that your parents are getting divorced and you get to watch them fight over you as though you are a part of the marital assets. We find out in different ways and at different times, but the message is always the same: life in the dash can be heaven one day and hell the next. Postmodern man still cries the ancient confession of Job:

> *How frail is man, how few his days, how full of trouble! He blossoms for a moment like a flower—and withers; as the shadow of a passing cloud, he quickly disappears.* (Job 14:1–2 TLB).

Life Is Lived Within a Series of Situations

Situations are created when you find yourself between the way things are and the way they ought to be.

Cancer is a situation. It is not the way it should be; that's why they call it disease. Divorce is a situation. The loss of a job is a situation. The death of child is a situation. A car accident—everything from a fender bender to a head-on collision—is a real-life, unavoidable, undeniable situation.

And while situations differ greatly in size and severity, the core choices they prompt always remain the same. Will this make me bitter or better? Will I be able to stand still long enough for God to show me the good that can come from this situation? Will I quit and resort to crawling or coasting, just because the prospect of climbing seems unbearable? The choice is always mine and mine alone to make. W. Clement Stone once noted, "To every disadvantage there is a corresponding advantage." And the apostle Paul said,

> *I know how to live on almost nothing or with everything. I have learned the secret of contentment in every situation, whether it be a full stomach or hunger, plenty or want; for I can do everything God asks me to with the help of Christ who gives me the strength and power.* (Phil. 4:12–13 TLB).

Paul claimed that in every situation, he had choices. What is it about one person that makes him stronger, more resolute, more loving, more faithful, and more compassionate the more the pressure is applied? And why can a seemingly similar set of circumstances do just the opposite for another?

A sixteen-year-old girl said to her father, "Daddy, my life is not one darn thing after another; it's one darn thing all the time. What am I going to do?" Her wise father took her to the kitchen. He placed three pans of water on the stove to boil. In one he placed a carrot, in one he placed an egg, and in one he placed ground coffee. After a few minutes he turned and explained, "Hot water has turned the carrot to mush and has turned the egg hard. You can let the hot water of hard times make you soft, as in the case of the carrot, or hard, as in the case of the egg." He then turned to the third pot, with the coffee. He continued, "Or you can change the water into something delightful, as in the case of the coffee. Coffee needs hot water to release its flavor and aroma. Honey—be the coffee!"

Hot water is not merely a fact of life; it is a necessity. Without it you will never fully be what God intended.

Life Is Lived Within a Series of Seasons

The Bible says it this way:

> *There is a time for everything, and a season for every activity under heaven: a time to be born and a time to die, a time to plant and a time to uproot, a time to kill and a time to heal, a time to tear down and a time to build, a time to weep and a time to laugh, a time to mourn and a time to dance.* (Eccl. 3:1–4 NIV)

The weather changes every season as spring turns into summer, summer into fall, and inevitably fall into winter. In a similar way, life moves from birth to growth, maturity, decline, and death. God ordained the whole process and it has been going on since Adam.

Like other things in life, most of us have a favorite season. Just about everybody likes spring and fall. Some live for the sweltering heat of the summer—but few love the winter when things lie dormant or dead.

Question: Is every season necessary? Answer: Yes! The trick is not to get your seasons confused.

Winter is a time of preparation. Spring is the time of planting. Summer is the time for plowing and weeding. Fall is the season of harvest, and even that one is regulated by what you've accomplished in the other three.

You can't afford to allow the bruises, the brokenness, or the boredom of where you are right now to rob you of the opportunity to respond constructively. What you do in the moments of your greatest loss and grief will determine whether there will be joy in the morning. How you respond in this season counts forever. So be wise. Ask yourself a few questions:

- Is this a downtime that God has given me in order to dream a new dream and make a new plan for a future? Sometimes we get so fixed on our losses that we overlook the new possibilities open to us.
- Is this a time to plow up new ground and plant new crops?
- Is this a time to keep faith and believe in what I've already planted?
- Is this weed choppin' time? If it is, then it's summer, and harvest is just around the corner.

We can still benefit today from the encouragement Paul gave the early Christians: "Let us not become weary in doing good, for at the proper time we will reap a harvest if we do not give up" (Gal. 6:9 NIV).

GET IN THE GAME!

Like it or not, life in the dash ceaselessly and inexorably moves from side to side, from situation to situation, and from season to season. The journey for some lasts longer than for others, but the travel is sure and the destination certain.

As Goethe, the eighteenth-century German poet, novelist, and scientist, said, "Art is long, life short; judgment difficult, opportunity transient." Each and every form of adversity brings a grand opportunity to be seized for those who know how.

Not long ago I watched my daughter Paige play in a soccer doubleheader. Well into the second game, the girls felt hot and tired. They had only one extra player, so substitutions came few and far between. One particular girl complained the entire game. She just stood around, flat-footed and whining about the heat and her fatigue and how long she had played. She wanted out. She needed a drink of water. *Take her out,* I thought, *just to get her to shut up!*

Just about that time, something strangely amazing happened. The same little girl with a litany of complaints got elbowed square in the mouth by one of her opponents who was attempting an end run with the ball. As her head snapped back, it was as though someone threw a switch in her head. She reached up to wipe the blood from her lip and I saw a look of determination cross her face. She lowered her head and took off after the offender as if her shoes had caught fire. She not only ran down her opponent and took her down, but she ran full out for the rest of the game. Her complaints evaporated in the heat of the battle and she became a player possessed, alert and fully engaged.

Now, I've seen others receive the same smack in the face who immediately slump down and cry. Why do some people thrive no matter what happens, while others merely try to survive? Is it talent? Breeding or background? While I am sure all these things help, they cannot fully explain why some develop a victim mentality and others, often with less advantage and more adversity, wind up victors. To find that answer, you have to reach beyond talent and background and get to attitude.

ATTITUDE DETERMINES ALTITUDE

Two verses from the Bible reveal why some people fail and others succeed. "As [a man] thinketh in his heart," says one, "so is he" (Prov. 23:7 KJV). The second reinforces the first: "Above all else, guard your heart, for it is the wellspring of life" (Prov. 4:23 NIV).

The key to your success or failure lies in the condition of your heart. Your attitude originates in your heart, and your power to choose resides in your attitude. Therefore, your attitude exposes the true you as either strong or weak. It reveals your inner integrity (or lack thereof). Your attitude is more honest and more consistent than your words. It can never be hidden for long and will always be expressed. It functions as the megaphone of your soul and predicts your future better than anything else. It can be your best friend or your worst enemy.

Attitude may not be everything, but I'm convinced it's as close as we'll ever get to understanding what separates winners from whiners and victors from victims. Attitude affects daily outcomes more than any other factor—more than intellect, more than talent, and more than privilege.

You can't change where you were born, your parents, or the family you were born into. You might be able to alter your appearance, but you can't trade in things like IQ and natural talents for a bigger, better version. Education and training can open some doors for you, but they cannot change your past, make you taller or more athletic, or alter the fact that some people will treat you unfairly.

Yet with the right attitude, you can turn adversity into an advantage. You have the power to use disappointment as the construction material for building patience. You can use opposition as an opportunity to develop perseverance. Danger can turn to courage and pain to gain, all through the power of a right attitude. You can't make people love you or keep their promises. You can't control the seasons of loss or suffering. But you can and must gain control of your attitude.

I have spent my life observing not only human nature, but also human performance, and I firmly embrace the sublime words of the Declaration of Independence:

> We hold these Truths to be self-evident, that all Men are created equal, that they are endowed by their Creator with certain unalienable Rights, that among these are Life, Liberty, and the Pursuit of Happiness. . . .

Are all men *really* created equal? Certainly, not all men are equally happy or good or productive or loving or strong. Anyone can see truly remarkable gaps between the lives of, say, a Hitler and a Mother Teresa. So if we believe all men are created equal, then how do we account for the differences among human beings in the quality and contributions of their lives?

As Benjamin Franklin concluded a stirring speech on the guarantees of the Constitution, a heckler shouted, "Aw, them words don't mean nothin' at all. Where's all the happiness you say it guarantees us?"

Franklin smiled and replied, "My friend, the Constitution guarantees the American people only the right to *pursue* happiness; you have to catch it yourself."

What separates those who "catch it" from those who merely and madly chase after it? Why do some people live amazing lives in their dash?

Under pressure, some people react emotionally, while others respond from a deep reserve of strength. Reactors are victims by definition. Responders are victors by choice. While victims are overcome by circumstances, victors overcome despite them. The first gives up power by reacting to events, while the second retains power by developing response-abilities. Victors transform their attitude into an ally. Victims wear their attitude like an anchor around their necks, dragging them down.

Attitudes come in two basic types: entitlement and gratitude. If you turn grief into gladness, your attitude has made the transformation possible. Attitude is everything in prevailing against adversity. As long as things remain rosy and sunny, anyone can fake a positive attitude; but under stress, the true condition of the heart comes to the surface—good or bad, weak or strong. Put a small and needy heart under pressure, and an attitude of entitlement emerges. Walk a person with a strong heart through hell, and you'll get an entirely different result.

The Crawler's Attitude: Entitlement

A crawler's attitude says, "You (and everyone else in the world) owe me." This attitude seeks its rights, with no thought to responsibilities.

Such an attitude fueled Satan's brazen attempt to lead a rebellion in heaven against the very throne of God, resulting in his expulsion. The same attitude drove Adam and Eve to openly defy God, resulting in their expulsion from the Garden of Eden. The most hellish and damning cast of mind harbored in the human heart is an attitude of entitlement. Consider it a spiritual virus, a corrosive and corrupting acid of the soul. It knows no joy, gives no peace, and allows for no redemption.

Think of the attitude of entitlement like an old, rusty anchor chained to a proud and arrogant man. It reveals a hollow heart that can never be filled and will never be satisfied. It prompts the insatiable drive for more and fosters the almost incurable belief that no matter what you have, it will never be enough. Though you may have all the trappings of success, you still feel empty. The most miserable people in the world are not those who have suffered great losses, but those who have everything they've ever wanted—except the power to enjoy it. One man who knew all about such tragedies wrote, "I have seen another evil under the sun, and it weighs heavily on men: God gives a man wealth, possessions and honor, so that he lacks nothing his heart desires, but God does not enable him to enjoy them, and a stranger enjoys them instead. This is meaningless, a grievous evil" (Eccl. 6:1–2 NIV).

Those who suffer from the attitude of entitlement have lost the ability to admire without a corresponding need to acquire. They have every reason to be thankful, but none of the power to be grateful. They know the price of everything, but the value of nothing. They consume everything without thinking of giving something back, not even a thank you. The person with an ungrateful heart believes that everything God does for him is too little and anything he does for God is too much. Entitlement is the cry of the orphaned soul and the abandoned heart.

And the only cure for the attitude of entitlement? An attitude of gratitude.

The Climber's Attitude: Gratitude

Those with a grateful heart can endure anything, even the loss of everything—even life itself.

Many years ago I watched an interview with a dying Arthur Ashe, the first African-American to win the Grand Slam of tennis. Ashe had contracted AIDS from a blood transfusion and the interviewer wondered if he ever felt tempted to ask, "God, why me?" Ashe responded without hesitation, "No, I never ask that question, because I didn't ask it when I was standing at Wimbledon holding the championship trophy over my head."

What an attitude! What a class act and what an example of a real winner. Ashe knew what the rest of us are still learning. He considered all of life a gift. The amazing talent that made him a tennis champion also made him a winner in the game of life. He felt grateful for what he had been given, not hateful for what he was losing. He loved life and savored each moment, even the ones he couldn't explain.

An attitude of gratitude can take a shabby garage apartment and turn it into a love nest. It can take a minimum-wage job and turn it into an opportunity of a lifetime. It can take the sad news of cancer and turn it into a journey of healing and discovery.

This kind of attitude is what made Job the poster child for climbers. When we first meet Job in the Bible, we find a fabulously wealthy and successful man with a large, loving family. He enjoyed the respect of his peers, the admiration of his family, the blessings of God . . . and the ire of the devil.

Satan saw Job as a fair-weather friend to God. He even challenged God to a contest, with Job as the guinea pig. Satan proposed that Job loved God only for what he had been given. If God allowed the stuff of Job's life to be stripped away, Satan claimed, Job would reveal his true heart and curse God. God allowed Job to be tested. Why? The New Testament tells us the purpose of such testing: "You know that under pressure, your faith-life is forced into the open and shows its true colors. So don't try to get out of anything prematurely. Let it do its work so you become mature and well-developed, not deficient in any way" (James 1:3–4 THE MESSAGE).

Even though God allowed Satan to test Job, he did set limits. Satan could strip Job of the stuff of his life, but not his life itself. God said, "Everything he has is in your hands, but on the man himself do not lay a finger" (Job 1:12 NIV). With the ground rules firmly in place, the test of Job's lifetime began. Four times in the span of one day Job heard bad news. First, it was all his oxen and servants—gone. Second, it was all his sheep and servants—gone. Third, it was all his camels and servants—gone. And finally, Job received word that all of his children—seven sons and three daughters—died in a freak accident of nature.

Who could imagine that the man described as the greatest among the people of the east could suffer the loss of his entire fortune and all ten of his children in one afternoon? But then Job did something totally weird by today's standards. The Bible says, "At this, Job got up and tore his robe and shaved his head. Then he fell to the ground in worship" (Job 1:20 NIV). I don't find the first two things Job did as at all odd.

People in Job's day customarily showed their grief like this, and Job was no different.

What strikes me as odd is his attitude. He fell to the ground, not in an attitude of anger or bitterness or even hatred, but of *worship*. Doesn't that seem an odd response to the loss of everything you had worked a lifetime to accumulate? Yet Job bowed low and worshiped God. What he said next revealed what only God could have known, and what Satan was so eager to find out. In a posture of humility and a spirit of gratitude, Job declared, "I came naked from my mother's womb, and I shall have nothing when I die. The Lord gave me everything I had, and they were his to take away. Blessed be the name of the Lord." And the Bible comments, "In all of this, Job did not sin or revile God" (Job 1:21–22 TLB).

Don't miss this cry from Job's heart. His confession in the midst of loss proved Satan to be what he has always been: a liar. Job actually *loved* God—imagine that! He didn't love God merely for his wealth and health, as Satan had suggested. He loved God for who he is and not merely for what he gave. Job considered everything he had as on loan from God. Job never adopted an owner's mentality. He knew that the gifts of God, no matter how near and dear, could never be allowed to take the place of God.

Job revealed in his loss what he believed in his gain. "God is the giver, and I am the receiver." Everything that God has given, life will one day take back. Nothing you have today has come to stay. The only permanent gift God has given you is the gift of himself and his relentless love. This fact had captured the heart of Job long before he became rich. Job turned his grief into gladness by choosing to be grateful rather than hateful.

Job believed in his lifetime what others have learned in theirs: "Every good and perfect gift is from above, coming down from the Father of the heavenly lights" (James 1:17 NIV). He also personified the biblical command to "give thanks in all circumstances, for this is God's will for you in Christ Jesus" (1 Thess. 5:18 NIV). God didn't ask him to give thanks for all that had happened. Job didn't feel glad at the loss of his wealth and health and children. But even in his grief, he could maintain his gladness. He grieved his losses—he wasn't superhuman—but he maintained a sober gladness of heart. He trusted that God would make sense of what seemed like a senseless situation. He believed God loved him, which meant that nothing could get to Job without first passing through the loving heart of God.

But make no mistake. The attitude of gratitude, which Job displayed, is neither easily achieved nor maintained. For the past thirty years as a pastor, I've seen the troubles of Job visited upon modern people. I have watched them wake up with everything in the morning and go to bed that night with nothing. I have seen believers with modest means turn loss into gladness as they celebrated the goodness of God in life and death. I have seen others with all the advantages of wealth and education fold under a crushing weight of sadness over the loss of what they always thought they deserved and never thought they'd lose.

People who adopt an attitude of gratitude don't stop believing in miracles when everyone around them has given up and taken the advice of Job's wife, "Curse God and die!" (Job 2:9 NIV).

Job's revolutionary response to his wife's advice reveals a great deal about him: "Shall we accept good from God, and not trouble?" (Job 2:10 NIV). Job believed that God ruled over all of life. He believed God to be both good and great. He knew in his heart that no one could take from him or keep from him what God wanted for him, but God alone. He believed that God could and would replace everything life had taken from him. Job's faith never wavered until he came under the influence of his so-called friends. It took three unrelenting friends, all with the attitude of entitlement, to plunge Job into a painful period of self-doubt and despair.

In the end, Job discovered that he had placed his faith in the right spot. At the end of the story he becomes twice as wealthy as before and "The Lord blessed the latter part of Job's life more than the first" (Job 42:2 NIV). Life can take nothing from a man whose heart remains anchored in God's love and therefore exhibits an attitude of gratitude.

During Rudyard Kipling's reign as England's most popular writer, the news got out that his publishers paid him a dollar a word for his work. Some Cambridge students, hearing this, cabled Kipling two dollars, along with instructions, "Please send us two of your very best words." To which Kipling replied in a telegram, "Thank you."

The secret to gaining a great heart is to say thank you, and often. "Thank you, God, for another day." "Thank you, God, for the gift of life and for the gift of my dash." And while it may be human nature to grumble at having to rise early in the morning until the day when you can't get up at all, I urge you to reject the attitude of entitlement. Trust God and be grateful; trust your stuff and be hateful. The choice is always and only yours.

Make the choice to see all of life as an amazing gift—even the hard parts.

3

Turning Rejection into Right Directions

Many of our fears are tissue-paper thin, and a single courageous step would carry us clear through them.

—BRENDAN FRANCIS

Have you ever done anything so dumb that you couldn't believe you actually did it? I have, more times than I'd like to remember. One of my most memorable mishaps occurred on my very first long-distance motorcycle trip.

The mother of a dear friend of mine was having surgery in Tupelo, Mississippi, and I decided to visit. Nashville, my home, lies exactly two hundred miles from Tupelo down a scenic road named the Natchez Trace, one of the most scenic roads in the South. Since it was mid-October, with mild temperatures and Technicolor leaves, this seemed the perfect time to break in my new Harley.

The ride down went nearly perfect. It bothered me a little that the scenery didn't change much—I'd expected a few more landmarks on the way down so I could gauge my progress on the way back up—but because the Trace goes basically north and south, I didn't think too much about it. *After all,* I thought, *there are only two ways to go—the right way and the wrong way.*

I made my visit, spent the night, and got up the next morning to set out for home. On the way down I'd determined that my first big landmark would be Tishomingo, Mississippi. After Tishomingo comes Alabama, then the Tennessee line, and then I'm almost home. But as I rode and rode, Tishomingo failed to show and I began to get more than a little nervous. After almost two hours had passed, I saw a sign that read, "Jackson, 46 miles."

"O God," I prayed, "let this be Jackson, Tennessee!"

It wasn't.

I had to accept that I had gone 120 miles in the wrong direction—leaving me 320 miles from home. By the time I realized what I'd done and turned around, I could have been home! I stopped, got off my bike and walked around it three or four times, just shaking my head. I was low on gas, short on time, and down on myself.

As I stood there, disgusted, a strange feeling came over me. I had felt something like it before, but never with anything of this intensity or to this degree of finality. I felt that I had gone too far to turn around—a weird, demonic, ill wind blowing across my soul. I kept hearing the same thing in my head over and over, getting louder and louder and becoming more believable and inevitable with each repetition: "You've gone too far to turn around!"

I listened for the voice of God. I prayed. I pleaded. I begged God to send down a holy helicopter to rescue me from where my own carelessness and arrogance had taken me. What a lonely, pathetic feeling swept over me that afternoon. I thought, *I can't make it from here.*

Have you ever felt as if you've gone too far to turn around and take the right road? You have only two choices when you find yourself heading in the wrong direction: turn around or keep going the wrong way. On that day I couldn't choose not to be where I was, but I could choose what I did next, from right where I was. I felt dumb and inferior. I felt like a reject. I wondered how God must feel, having made such a foolish fellow. But I changed my aptitude and took control of my actions. I turned around and headed in the right direction.

At that backwoods place I learned again that you can go farther than you think you can and you can turn around at any place to start back the right way. And when feelings of rejection come, you can either turn them in the right direction or you can continue going the wrong way, headed for all the wrong places.

THE INEVITABILITY OF REJECTION

Rejection demoralizes. It is bad enough to feel rejected by others; it is even worse to feel you have done something so dumb that you don't even like yourself.

The fact of rejection evokes corresponding feelings of worthlessness. And some pretty surprising individuals have felt such a wicked sting.

- After the great dancer Fred Astaire took his first screen test in 1933, the testing director of MGM wrote a memo that said of him, "Can't act! Slightly bald! Can dance only a little!" Astaire kept that memo over the fireplace in his Beverly Hills home and used it as motivation to prove people wrong.
- One expert reportedly said that Vince Lombardi "possesses *minimal* football knowledge and lacks motivation."
- Someone encouraged Louisa May Alcott, the author of *Little Women,* to find work as a servant or seamstress—anything but try to write.
- Beethoven handled a violin awkwardly and preferred to play his own compositions. His teacher labeled him hopeless as a composer.
- A newspaper editor fired Walt Disney for lack of ideas; the creator of Mickey Mouse also went bankrupt several times before he built Disneyland.
- Thomas Edison's teachers labeled him as too stupid to learn anything.
- Albert Einstein did not speak until he was four years old and didn't read until he was seven. His teachers described him as "mentally slow, unsociable, and adrift forever in his foolish dreams." In 1905, the University of Bern turned down his Ph.D. dissertation as being irrelevant and fanciful.

- Sir Isaac Newton did poorly in grade school.
- Leo Tolstoy, author of *War and Peace,* flunked out of college and there won the description of being both "unable and unwilling to learn."
- Henry Ford failed and went broke five times before he finally succeeded.
- Winston Churchill failed the sixth grade, and in 1894, the rhetoric teacher at Harrow in England wrote on this sixteen-year-old's report card, "a conspicuous lack of success." After a lifetime of defeats and setbacks, Churchill finally got elected prime minister of England—but not until he reached the age of sixty-two.
- In 1902 the poetry editor of the *Atlantic Monthly* returned a sheaf of poems to a twenty-eight-year-old poet named Robert Frost with this curt note: "Our magazine has no room for your vigorous verse."

Today, no one would consider these people rejects, even though they faced their share of rejection. All of us, at some time, feel ordinary, stupid, and rejected. These are common adversities. The difference between those who push on to greatness and those who quit and settle for less is the ability to turn rejections in the right directions.

People reject other people all the time for the most ridiculous reasons. Adults reject other adults because they do not belong to the "right" political party, civic club, or because they live in the "wrong" neighborhood. I've seen ex-jocks huddle in their closed groups to relive old sports stories, consciously excluding those with no glorious sporting past. Women divide into those who shop exclusively at the designer boutiques and those who shop only at thrift and discount stores. Teens reject other teens for wearing style-less shoes, flare-less jeans, and even vogue-less haircuts.

Rejection is unavoidable. The question is not, will you be rejected, but what will you do when you face it? Will you accept it and play the role of a victim? Or will you reject the rejection?

WHERE THE WAR BEGAN

Since rejection is a universal experience, I've often wondered, "Where did this war begin?" I've found the answer in the Bible.

According to the Scriptures, the DNA of rejection gets passed down to us from our parents, who got it from their parents, who got it from our first parents—Adam and Eve. They rebelled against God in the Garden of Eden, and as a consequence, rejection has reverberated through every generation since, robbing us of peace and power.

The Scriptures tell us, "All we like sheep who have gone astray; we have all turned to our own way" (Isa. 53:6 NRSV). The wisest man who ever lived, Solomon, said that God "has also set eternity in the hearts of men; yet they cannot fathom what God has done from beginning to end" (Eccl. 3:11 NIV). All of us have a God-shaped vacuum at the center of our hearts, and nothing will fill that void except a vital, ongoing relationship with him. Without it, you can feel only flawed and phony. And because God loves you, he will not allow anyone or anything else to fill up the space in your heart that was made for him alone.

What is the right direction to turn when faced with rejection? Turn to God. He alone knows your true worth and potential. He alone has promised to be your help, your refuge, and your strong tower. He alone knows your true destiny. And he alone can give you boldness on the journey of life.

The Bible declares, "The wicked man flees though no one pursues, but the righteous are as bold as a lion" (Prov. 28:1 NIV). Without God, our lives are but a whimper, but with God, we can live as boldly as a lion. We were made to roar! We can roar because we have something to say, something to do, and something that only we can contribute.

But because we don't like what we see when we come face-to-face with our true humanity—as I did going the wrong way on a two-way road—we think it stands to reason that God couldn't possibly like what he sees in us. After all, he is God, and he sees and knows everything. He is flawless and I am flawed. He is perfect and I am everything but.

These feelings are painfully real. But they also reveal lies that need to be exposed and expelled. Without such an exposure and expulsion, we'll wind up feeling we've wandered too far the wrong way to turn around.

THE ANATOMY OF REJECTION

Adam and Eve lived in a perfect environment that afforded them constant contact with God. They were emotionally, intellectually, and spiritually intact, in touch, and in tune with God. It had never occurred to them to question God's instructions or his intentions. But with a nudge from Satan, Adam and Eve did what they had never done before—mistrusted God. Through that single act of sinful suspicion, the DNA of fear and rejection was passed down to us.

Rejection: The Fear of Being Exposed

Mistrust and paranoia are not only in the air, but in our blood. After Adam and Eve ate from the Tree of the Knowledge of Good and Evil, they did what they had never felt the need to do—they hid. When God came to commune with them, they vanished into the foliage.

As he walked in the Garden, God inquired, "Adam, where are you?" Adam whispered, "I heard you coming and didn't want you to see me naked, so I hid."

If I were God, I would have asked, "Why did you hide?" But God asked a more piercing question: "Who told you that you were naked?"

We could benefit from similar questions today. "Who told you that you were not good enough?" "Who told you that you are an accident?" "Who told you that you don't measure up?" "Who told you you've gone too far to turn around?" "Who told you that you're the only one who has ever felt this way?" These questions, and a thousand like them, serve to remind us that God sees things differently than we do.

Yet they also may cause us to lock onto our liabilities like a laser. Since the fall of our first parents, we all feel the need to hide and cover up for what we've done. Guilt and inferiority have become our most abundant fears, with separation and suspicion their only fruit.

On the one hand, guilt is not a bad thing, since it is a God thing. We ought to feel pain over doing what we ought not to have done, or over failing to do what we should have done. God uses guilt to stop us from going the wrong way and to turn us the right way. Guilt, from God's perspective, is a loving act and an effective force to bring about needed change. While it brings God no pleasure to cause us pain—the Lord "does not willingly bring affliction or grief to the children of men," says Jeremiah (Lam. 3:33 NIV)—real guilt is a form of grace. It is God's way of letting us know that we're going the wrong way.

Listen to God's gracious promise: "He who conceals his sins does not prosper, but whoever confesses and renounces them finds mercy" (Prov. 28:13 NIV). Without feelings of guilt, we would never know the greatness of grace.

But guilt denied and covered soon turns into shame. The Greek philosopher Seneca said it this way: "Every guilty person is his own hangman." Shame is the pain you feel, not for what you've done, but for who you have become. When we do wrong, we're scared to death of being exposed and found out, so we often settle for denying that we are on the wrong road, far from home. That's too bad, because in God's eyes, it is never too late to come clean and turn around. The biblical word *repent* literally means "to change your mind," with the connotation of doing a 180 in order to head back toward God. The apostle Paul commended the believers at Thessalonica because they "turned to God from idols to serve the living and true God" (1 Thess. 1:9 NIV). God offers to forgive us and cleanse our hearts—but we can't until we come clean. And we won't come clean as long as we hide.

Rejection: The Fear of Being Expelled

God expelled Adam and Eve from the Garden of Eden and placed angelic guards around the perimeter to prevent them from reentering their custom-made home (Gen. 3:23–24)—a home they gave up for a bite of some stupid fruit.

And so Adam and Eve became something God never intended them to be: nomads. That's why even today we all feel so profoundly lonely. That's why we long for home. As the theme song for the former hit TV sitcom *Cheers* says, we all long for a place, "where everyone knows your name and everyone is glad you came." We are all looking for a place where we're loved and accepted.

Maybe that is what Thoreau meant when he described city life as "millions of people living together alone." Isn't it ironic that we call some buildings "apartments"? Shouldn't they be called "attachments"? Wherever we live or however we live, we all face the fear of rejection that comes from being shut out and marginalized. We long to get on the road that leads home.

Recently I read an article in which the great, legendary golfer Arnold Palmer announced that he would be playing his last Masters Tournament in 2002. Palmer, who won the Masters in '58, '60, '62, and '64, is considered one of the greatest golfers in history. Yet Palmer said he planned to drop out of the prestigious tournament before the tournament dropped him. *USA Today* said,

> Even if Palmer wanted to keep going, Augusta National might have balked. Already, the club sent letters to three former champions—Doug Ford, Gay Brewer, and Billy Casper—recommending they stop playing this year. All complied, but not without some hurt feelings. "I don't want to get a letter," Palmer quipped.[1]

No one likes to hear that they've become irrelevant. The directors of Augusta National might have celebrated Palmer in 1964, but not in 2002, when players like Tiger Woods dominated the course. In this world, glory fades *fast*. Not even sports superstars are immune to rejection.

I vividly remember the first time I felt rejected. In high school I wanted to associate with the "in" group and sit at the jocks' table at lunchtime. All the cheerleaders sat at one table, the nerds sat at another, and the rednecks grabbed their own table. The greasers and motorheads gathered way in the back and spent their time either cleaning their fingernails or playing with the cigarettes lodged behind their ears. Each day as I entered the cafeteria I prayed, "Lord, let the right group make room for me today!" I never did sit with the jocks.

Everyone remembers what it's like to be passed over for the team. The real revelation came for me the day I realized that it doesn't get much better beyond high school. Feelings of rejection await us at every turn. We constantly hear that we are too old or too young or too smart or too dumb or too early or too late; it's always something.

But God wants to use these common experiences of rejection to turn us to him. He allows us to feel rejected by others in order to seek the only acceptance that matters: his!

Too often we fear rejection by others more than we fear God. Although the Bible says that the fear of God is the beginning of wisdom

(Prov. 9:10), we settle for a life of fearing people. I've noticed that we tend to fear people in at least one of four ways.

First, we fear what people will think of us. It's like the teenage boy who said to his mother, "Mama, I want to dress different, like everyone else."

Second, we fear what people may say about us. Will they like our clothes, our personalities, and our performances?

Third, we fear what people might do to us. Will they throw rocks? Embarrass us in front of others?

Last, we fear what people might fail to do *for* us. Will they conveniently forget to introduce us at an important event? Will they neglect to fulfill their promises?

These four fears will tie us into knots, steal our joy, and sap our hopes for significance—if we let them.

It is true that these fears grow and multiply because we live in a fast-paced world whose favorite questions are, "What have you done for me lately?" "What is your next hit?" "When is your newest thing coming out?" Because we buy into this backward way of thinking, we live in fear. And even if everything we did succeeded, we would grow even more fearful. We have many excuses for feeling bad:

"You know, if you were this dumb, you would feel this bad, too."

"If you had a lousy job like me, you'd feel this bad, too."

"If you'd been treated as badly and wronged as long as me, you'd feel twice as bad as I do now."

A great way to feel worse than you do right now is to grow jealous of the person who you think has it made. Guess what? He or she feels jealous of you. Bottom line—nothing in this world is ever going to fill you up, raise your worth, or love you back, except God. Get that truth straight in your mind. Only a vital, vibrant relationship with a personal, powerful God can meet your deepest needs. A wonderfully loving husband can't do it. A giving, gracious wife can't do it. Thank God that you have a great mom, a great dad, and great kids. But at the end of the day, they cannot satisfy your primary need. What we want is someone who knows us intimately and loves us unconditionally. We dare dream of someone who loves us most when we deserve it least. We need someone who can bring us home and keep us safe. Only God promises to do that, and only he can pull it off.

God wants to love you, but you must let him. You do not embarrass God, but you remain cut off from him until you claim this promise: "Here I am! I stand at the door and knock. If anyone hears my voice and opens the door, I will come in and eat with him, and he with me" (Rev. 3:20 NIV). God will not come into your life uninvited. He may ride the storms and rule the seas. He may have scooped out the valleys with his hands and piled up the mountains with his word, but he refuses to change a human heart without permission.

So the real question is, why would anyone hold God off when he offers us everything?

TWO GRACIOUS PROMISES

What is so special about God's offer of grace? Study the Scriptures from front to back, distill all the commands, covenants, and the direct statements of God, and you will see two primary themes. First, whatever you uncover to God, God will cover up with his love. And second, whatever you come clean about, God will convert into something holy and healthy.

Whatever You Uncover, God Will Cover

With an offer like this, why hide? Why settle for a skin-deep covering when we can come totally clean with God and find forgiveness and freedom?

Whatever we uncover about our sin—our fear, pain, or feelings of rejection—he will cover with his love and grace. Still, exposing our true selves, especially to God, is not easy. Even though God says that "all our righteousnesses are filthy rags" (Isa. 64:6 KJV), we fear to undress in front of him. So we mistakenly believe that if we cover our sorrow and sin in self-made robes of righteousness, God won't be able to see the emptiness and hollowness inside. When you were a kid, didn't you sometimes tell a lie when the truth would have worked just as well? But today is turning-around time. It's time to grow up by refusing to act as though nothing's wrong. And remember, whatever you uncover, God will cover.

He certainly went into the covering business for Adam and Eve. "The

Lord God clothed Adam and his wife with garments made from skins of animals," the Bible says (Gen. 3:21 TLB). This is the first place in Scripture that alludes to the idea of the shedding of blood in order to cover our guilt. God shed the blood of animals to cover Adam and Eve, and so started the long journey for God and man that reached an awful crescendo with Jesus Christ hanging on a cross to become our permanent sin covering.

God says to us today, "You know what I'll do? If you'll uncover and simply come clean, then I'll cover your sin and shame with my love and grace." What good news this is! No wonder Jesus said that all of heaven rejoices whenever one person turns around and begins a journey back to God (Luke 15:7).

Whatever You Confess, God Will Convert

The apostle John wrote these life-giving words: "If we confess our sins, he is faithful and just and will forgive us our sins and purify us from all unrighteousness" (1 John 1:9 NIV). The word *confess* in this verse literally means "to say the same thing again."

Confession is simply coming clean with what God already knows to be true about you. Confession requires the courage to come clean with God by simply calling sin what it is. If you have lied, call it what it is: a lie. If you have stolen the reputation of another through gossip, then call it what it is: sinful.

God responds to confession with cleansing. God loves it when we step out from behind our masks to tell the truth. Confession unlocks our broken hearts to all the good things God already has offered us in Christ. Through confession I get God's grace, his power, and his blessings—and all his promises become operational in my life!

The Bible makes it plain and simple. Consider God's contract with you: "Everyone who calls, 'Help, God!' gets help" (Rom. 10:13 THE MESSAGE). Think of that! Have you ever said to yourself, "I know I'm not perfect"? Whoever said you were? And, more important, whoever said that you needed to be? The truth is, I'm not okay and you're not okay, but that's okay, because the God who made us and loves us still loves us and always will. Everything that God has done in Christ screams, "You are loved!" So why do we think we still need to earn his love, when God's free gift is grace? Your past is not your future if the love of God reigns in your heart.

God's offer is grace for garbage and salvation for sin. A great deal! But it sounds too good to be true . . . and maybe that's why a lot of people remain un-confessed and undercover. It is a lot to believe that God, my Creator, wants to clean up my garbage—but he does! So here's the deal. Whatever I uncover, God covers. Whatever I confess, God cleans up. So why not come clean and confess that you need a Savior? You do that in real time by making the following confessions from the heart.

I'M ACCEPTED, THEREFORE I'M CONFIDENT

I know that God is my source and my strength. He's the lover of my soul and nothing or no one will ever change that.

God knows everything about me and loves me anyway. He accepts me unconditionally. He approves of me. Who else do I have to please and what else do I need to prove? I know God deeply loves me, so I can rest in that love for the rest of my life. "Accept each other just as Christ has accepted you," Paul said (Rom. 15:7 NLT).

Make this promise of Proverbs your own: "The wicked flee when no one is chasing them! But the godly are bold as lions" (28:1 TLB). The wicked flee because they feel paranoid; the godly are bold because they know God has plans for them. They have nothing hidden and nothing unsaid between them and God. They feel confident because they feel accepted. Their tears of confession have carried them to the depth of God's love. They know his fullness because they have confessed their emptiness. They enjoy God's acceptance without their rejection, his forgiveness without their failure, our togetherness without dreadful loneliness.

I AM ADOPTED, THEREFORE I AM COURAGEOUS

I'm a member of God's family, a child of the King. I'm a heavenly prince!

I have three children. Do you know who's my favorite? All of 'em! All of them are my babies. In the same way, if you're God's child, you're his favorite. He loves you.

Some of the greatest people in the Bible were adopted. Moses was adopted. The most courageous woman in the Bible, Esther, was adopted. Jesus was adopted by Joseph, since Mary was a virgin when she conceived by the power of God's Spirit. As a believer, I, too, am adopted into God's family. The Bible puts it this way: "For you did not receive a spirit that makes you a slave again to fear, but you received the Spirit of sonship. And by him we cry, 'Abba, Father'" (Rom. 8:15 NIV).

I've been with people who've gone through the adoptive process. It has to rank as one of the most amazing, thrilling experiences I've ever had. To see a man and a woman stand and look at a child who is not their own, and say, "Of all the children in the world, I choose you. Everything I have is yours. I will die for you. I will pour out my life for you."

That's what God did for us in Jesus Christ. So should we ever hesitate to call him Daddy? Should it be thought strange that we use his name? Tonya Donnelly, the lead singer of the punk group Belly, said in an interview with *Rolling Stone,* "For some reason, God is embarrassing to people. It doesn't embarrass somebody to talk about how they got completely bombed the night before, and puked all over themselves. But God, it seems, is a really embarrassing subject. How strange!" It's strange only to people outside the family. To me it doesn't feel strange at all. Do you know why? Because he's my dad!

I HAVE ACCESS, THEREFORE I'M CONTENTED

As a resident of Nashville—Music City USA—on several occasions I've hit the road with music artists. When the band and crew first arrive at a venue, they pass out "all access" backstage passes. Show your pass and you can go anywhere.

I love visiting friends who live in gated communities and they give me the private code. The door opens and I go through, strutting. I'm invited!

Listen to this: "So let us come boldly to the very throne of God and stay there to receive his mercy and to find grace to help us in our times of need" (Heb. 4:16 TLB).

Let me tell you the two greatest prayers you can ever utter. The first is, "Help!" To that prayer God says, "Good! I've been trying to make you miserable enough to abandon all your efforts of self-salvation. *Finally,* we can get down to the loving, lifelong relationship for which you were created!" The second is, "Thank you." Because anytime you cry, "Help!" I promise you, in God's name, you will have abundant reason to say, "Thank you."

ALL GOD ASKS

Ask God to penetrate the deep places of your life, where you most fear rejection. In this world of measurements and ample reasons to feel rejected, we can walk with a sense of confidence that we stand accepted by God, in Jesus Christ. That acceptance comes not as a result of our performance, but as a result of God's love. And all God asks in return is that we uncover and confess him as our Savior, the lover of our souls.

All of us have taken wrong turns. All of us have done profoundly stupid things for which we have no rational excuse. During those moments, we don't like ourselves very much. Yet it is in our lowest moments that we can experience the highest form of God's love, his grace. You can never wander so far down the wrong road that God can't find you where you are and bring you home.

4

Turning Jealousy into Joy

No man is a failure who is enjoying life.

—WILLIAM FEATHER

While vacationing with my family on the Oregon coast a few summers ago, I had my first experience of open-air fish markets. I didn't know that "fresh" seafood meant that most of it would still be alive and kicking.

I found it especially odd how they displayed live crabs. Not one of the markets we visited placed tops on the crab baskets. This seemed strange, especially as they were constantly climbing over each other and up the sides of the baskets. Out of curiosity, I asked one of the fishermen, "Why are there no tops on the crab baskets?"

"There's no need," he explained. "If one of the crabs starts to climb up the sides of the basket, the other crabs will reach up and pull it back down. The crabs are so selfish that they make sure no one will ever escape."

That sounds a lot like human behavior! I've often seen people behave like crabs; maybe that's where the phrase "Don't be crabby" originated. On a more sophisticated level we call this type of behavior jealousy.

Jealousy is a miserable, miserly feeling. This toxic emotion says, "What you have should be mine and I'm going to take it if I can, but if I can't, I'll make it hard for either of us to be happy." This deep-soul infection bleeds over and stains all of life. And no one under its spell can feel the least inkling of joy, because these two emotions cancel each other out.

Jealousy—the worst of all emotions—occurs when we fail to know who we are and what we're worth. It makes finding contentment and satisfaction impossible. Joy, on the other hand—the best of all human emotions—can't be fabricated, but only expressed. It ranks above mere happiness, because happiness depends on what happens. Joy rises from a heart that feels loved. That's why Nehemiah said, "The joy of the LORD is your strength." (Neh. 8:10 NIV). Not my bank account, not my degree, not my pedigree, not my job, not my position in the community—*the joy of the Lord* is my strength.

One cannot separate joy from God. When we realize we were made for a loving, lifelong relationship with God, then we discover we were created for joy. God, a creative genius, designed us with the capacity to enjoy great love as well as express it to others. Therefore the person who feels loved lives with gratitude, and gratitude knows nothing but joy. The empty person feels entitled to more and thus knows nothing but jealousy toward those who have what he thinks he deserves. The jealous person never experiences joy, and the joyful person has a natural immunity to jealousy. Jealousy makes us feel unloved, unwanted, unrecognized, or under-rewarded.

THE INNER VOICE OF JEALOUSY

Jealousy is like a low-level hum in your ears, like hearing voices of dissatisfaction deep down in your soul that refuse to be stilled and cannot be satisfied. At times, jealousy will feel like a low-grade fever; at others, like a raging paranoia that robs you of rest. It creates a restless tension full of whispered lies that, if repeated often enough, sound real. Sometimes it sounds like background noise, faint and constant, but other times it erupts like a marching band blaring out in Dolby stereo, "You deserve more and they deserve less!"

"You Deserve More, So Go and Get It"

Jealousy starts as a little voice in the back of your mind that says, "You deserve more than you have. You need to go out and get it. You need to get more, because other people are out there getting all the good stuff, and if you don't hurry, there won't be anything left."

Jealousy whispers, "Piling stuff on top of stuff is the key to life." Sure, you may already own a home, a car, and lots of stuff to plug into the wall, but jealousy insists, "You need just a little more." Jealousy craves more stuff to fill up the gaping hole in your heart created by the empty feeling that you are unworthy of love. Jealousy promises that if you could just get a newer car or a bigger house or a better apartment or a more beautiful spouse or a better job and a better class of friends, then you'd be really happy and truly joyful.

The Bible does not see things that way. "For wherever there is jealousy or selfish ambition," it says, "there will be disorder and every other kind of evil" (James 3:16 TLB). Untold varieties of evil come from that little voice that craves more stuff, bigger stuff, better stuff.

"They Deserve Less, So Go Take It"

As if one voice weren't bad enough, jealousy comes in stereo. No sooner do you hear, "You don't have what you deserve; you need to go get it," than a second voice chimes in, "They have more than they deserve, and you need to go take it."

I was born and reared in a small town in Barren County. When the early settlers looked for a name to describe their new home, they could come up with no better word than *barren*. It may be just a coincidence that I grew up in Barren County, but I felt barren for most of my childhood. I felt like the poster child for the average and the ordinary, like a beige individual in a brightly colored world. I learned early to feel "not-good-enough." Every authority figure in my adolescence felt duty-bound to remind me that I'd never done enough, loved enough, or worked hard enough.

This all changed for me when I met someone who told me that I could find real joy not in always getting what I wanted, but in letting go of what I didn't need. Jesus taught me that "a man's life does not consist in the abundance of his possessions" (Luke 12:15 NIV).

Jealousy bears a dehumanizing fruit called bitterness. Note how the Bible explains its toxic effect: "Watch out that no bitterness takes root among you, for as it springs up it causes deep trouble, hurting many in their spiritual lives" (Heb. 12:15 TLB).

An ancient story tells of the devil crossing the Libyan Desert. He came upon a number of small fiends tormenting a holy hermit. The devil watched as the saintly man easily shook off their evil suggestions. Finally, Satan stepped forward to offer advice. "What you do is too crude," he said. "Permit me for one moment."

Then he leaned over and whispered in the holy man's ear, "Your brother has just been made bishop of Alexandria." A scowl of jealousy suddenly clouded the serene face of the hermit.

"That," said the devil to his imps, "is the sort of thing that I recommend."

Jealousy whispers, "You would have what you deserve if all the other people weren't hogging it all." It is not enough that I succeed; everyone else must fail. But while jealousy takes aim at another, it wounds only itself.

Jealousy Is Like Heartburn of the Soul

Jealousy is to love what ashes are to flame; once it may have been part of the fire, but now it exists only to smother the flame and keep it smoldering.

The heartburn that jealousy produces comes from two basic sources: guilt and inferiority. I call them the GI Blues. David referred to this when he cried out, "O God, wash me, cleanse me from this guilt. Let me be pure again. For I admit my shameful deed—it haunts me day and night" (Ps. 51:2–3 TLB). Notice that he said, "It haunts me." Guilt and inferiority are twin fears. They function in the spirit like the smell of rotten eggs, warning of the presence of something that could explode if not detected and controlled. What Shakespeare wrote so eloquently in sixteenth-century England remains true today:

O, beware, my lord, of jealousy! It is the green-ey'd monster which doth mock the meat it feeds on.

An old French proverb says, "Jealousy is nourished by doubt." No more potent a fertilizer for jealousy exists than self-doubt. It can find an excuse to feel miserable in the face of the most wonderful circumstances. It creates its own private hell, regardless of what's going on outside. Left unchecked, jealousy will rob you of your relationships, your potential, your health, your peace, and the glory of the world around you. It will eat away your happiness like cancer consumes a diseased liver. And the fear it creates lives deep in each of us.

JOY IS YOUR STRENGTH

Joy is the only known cure for jealousy. And we can be glad that the Bible has much to recommend about its therapeutic power.

No language has as many words for joy and rejoicing as does Old Testament Hebrew. Ancient Hebrew has thirteen root terms for joy, used in twenty-seven different words, all of which express some aspect of joyful, thankful worship.

Hebrew religious ritual proclaimed God as the source of all joy. In contrast to the rituals of other faiths, Israelite worship came down to a joyous celebration. The good Israelite regarded the act of thanking God as the supreme joy of life. Pure joy has God as both its source and object. The psalmist says, "You show me the path of life. In your presence there is fullness of joy; in your right hand are pleasures forevermore" (Ps. 16:11 NRSV).

And yet, we should never confuse joy for mere pleasure. C. S. Lewis wrote, "I doubt whether anyone who has tasted joy would ever, if both were in his power, exchange it for all the pleasure in the world."[1]

Joy is to the heart and soul what the 1941 discovery of penicillin was to the body. Since the introduction of penicillin and the host of antibiotics that followed in its wake, the average life span of every boy, girl, man, and woman on the face of the planet has increased at least ten years!

Joy results from taking God and his promises seriously, and at the same time, not taking my current conditions or myself too seriously.

God replaces grim looks with great laughter. I consider laughter to be just as much a sign of a deep, maturing faith as looks of grave seriousness seem to be for some. Trying to live without laughter would be like driving a car with no springs: you'd feel every pothole and every annoying rock on the road. Why live like that? Joyless living is as uncomfortable as it is unnecessary, for joy is God's free gift to us—here and now.

I had the privilege to hear Stephane Grappelli, the world-renowned French violinist, perform at the end of his long and illustrious career. I felt pure joy just listening to him play. The experience reminded me of a story I heard many years ago about a poor old violinist whose playing brought great joy to everyone who heard him. An interviewer asked him why his music evoked such a response in his listeners. He pondered the question and then said, "Ah, a great deal of sunshine must have gone into this wood, and what has gone in comes out."

Joy comes from within. It is the fruit of a heart both loved and satisfied. And it is one of God's best gifts.

Joy Is Like Good Medicine

The Scriptures teach, "A cheerful heart is good medicine, but a crushed spirit dries up the bones" (Prov. 17:22 NIV). In *The Anatomy of an Illness,* Norman Cousins tells of lying in the hospital with a rare, crippling disease. When doctors diagnosed him as incurable, Cousins checked out of the hospital. Aware of how negative emotions can injure the body, Cousins reasoned that the reverse must also be true. So he borrowed a movie projector and prescribed his own treatment, consisting of Marx Brothers films and old *Candid Camera* reruns. It didn't take long for him to discover that ten minutes of laughter provided two hours of pain-free sleep.

Amazingly, Cousins eventually defeated his debilitating disease. After the account of his victory appeared in the *New England Journal of Medicine,* Cousins received more than three thousand letters from appreciative physicians throughout the world.

What lesson can we learn? Of all virtues, joy has the most immediate payoff. It makes the person who displays it happy. It can turn the most homely face radiant and winsome. It promotes health to the body, alertness to the mind, and brings fair weather to the soul. It telegraphs to everyone that something good on the inside is bursting to get out and scream at the top of its lungs.

Joy Screams, "I'm Cured!"

Joy erupts when someone believes that he or she has just overcome some virulent disease. And we all have a disease that causes dis-ease.

Mark Twain once said, "Man is the only animal that blushes. Or needs to." Who doesn't feel ashamed of things they've done in the past? Nobody who feels unforgiven and unforgiving can live in freedom. By contrast, joy screams, "I am cured! I am no longer held down by those awful feelings of guilt and inferiority!"

C. S. Lewis described happiness more than fifty years ago in terms that make even more sense today in our commuter-driven society:

A car is made to run on petrol [gasoline], and it would not run properly on anything else. Now God designed the human machine to run on himself. He himself is the fuel our spirits were designed to burn, or the food our spirits were designed to feed on. There is no other. That is why it is just no good asking God to make us happy in our own way without bothering about religion. God cannot give us a happiness and peace apart from himself, because it is not there. There is no such thing.[2]

How do we naturally respond when we see God? We feel convicted of sin. "Woe to me! . . . I am ruined!" confessed Isaiah after seeing the glory of God (Isa. 6:5 NIV). The closer I walk with God, the more quickly I feel my sin and realize how much I need him. It's like standing at a distance from a mirror. I look pretty good from across the room; my suit looks in order, my tie looks straight, and my hair looks combed. But as I move closer to the glass, my imperfections show up. I notice a spot on my suit, my tie looks wrinkled, and my hair seems out of place. The same things happen under the glare of bright lights. Blemishes and bulges hidden in the shadows stand out in the light. The more light we have, the more we see our defects. It's the same way when we get close to

God. When we draw near to him, we realize how much we need him and how far we have drifted from him.

Paul Tillich, a Lutheran theologian suspended by Hitler from the University of Frankfurt for his opposition to the war, had this to say about joy:

> Joy has something within itself that is beyond joy and sorrow. This something is called blessedness . . . [and] is asked for and promised in the Bible. It makes the joy of life possible in pleasure and pain, in happiness and unhappiness, in ecstasy and sorrow. Where there is joy, there is fulfillment. And where there is fulfillment, there is joy.[3]

The apostle Paul cried out for a cure for his undone-ness, "What a wretched man I am!" he wrote. "Who will rescue me from this body of death? Thanks be to God—through Jesus Christ our Lord! So then, I myself in my mind am a slave to God's law, but in the sinful nature a slave to the law of sin. Therefore, there is now no condemnation for those who are in Christ Jesus" (Rom. 7:24–8:1 NIV).

Our Lord Jesus Christ won joy for us through his suffering and sacrifice. And why did Christ willingly suffer as our Savior? The Bible explains: "Let us fix our eyes on Jesus, the author and perfecter of our faith, who for the joy set before him endured the cross, scorning its shame" (Heb. 12:2 NIV). There can be no joy without pain. In this way we learn that joy and pain go together. As Clyde Reid says in his book *Celebrate the Temporary:*

> One of the most common obstacles to celebrating life fully is our avoidance of pain. We do everything to escape pain. Our culture reinforces our avoidance of pain by assuring us that we can live a painless life. Advertisements constantly encourage us to believe that life can be pain-free. But to live without pain is a myth. To live without pain is to live half a life, without fullness of life. This is an unmistakable, clear, unalterable fact. Many of us do not realize that pain and joy run together. When we cut ourselves off from pain, we have unwittingly cut ourselves off from joy as well.[4]

A cable TV series about modern-day gangsters has struck a chord with a record number of viewers. *The Sopranos* boasts a weekly audience of tens of millions. According to James Gandolfini, who plays New Jersey mob boss Tony Soprano, "We show people sometimes being at their worst and regretting it. And people identify with that because we've all had times when we were at our worst."[5] What joy we can have in knowing that God loved us at our worst. He offers us his best for our worst!

Joy Is Like Good News

Because I love "good-news people" and avoid as much as possible "bad-news people," I thank God for caller ID. I can look at who's calling me and predict why they're calling.

We have enough real bad news in the world; I don't have time for those who want to make up more of it. Yet, since bad news sells, the media feel compelled to put a negative spin on everything, even good news. Want an example? Consider a headline from the *Washington Post* that ran in February 2002: "US Economy Gains, Adds 400,000 Jobs in One Month: Report Spurs Fears." Most people consider job growth good news; the *Post* warned that it could lead to increased interest rates. And when job growth slowed a couple of months later, the *New York Times* reported it as "Stirring Concern." The *Wall Street Journal* once warned that a weak dollar would drive away foreign investors and threaten our economy. Later, when the dollar grew strong, the *New York Times* cried that rapid growth prevents us from being able to "maintain economic stability in the foreign-exchange market."

These examples prove that you can put a negative spin on anything, even good news. On the other hand, you can find something good in any situation . . . if you look. Remember, it's always your choice.

I agree with Albert Einstein, who said, "I want to know God's thoughts . . . the rest are details." And I want to know if God has any good news for this bad-news world.

Victor Hugo said, "The supreme happiness of life is the conviction that we are loved." We all want to be wanted. We long for someone who knows us thoroughly and loves us completely. We need someone to love us preemptively, accept us unconditionally, and believe in our potential. We desire someone who knows where we've been, what we've done, how we've behaved, and who yet remains enthusiastic about our future. Jesus expressed it this way:

> *Come to me and I will give you rest—all of you who work so hard beneath a heavy yoke. Wear my yoke—for it fits perfectly—and let me teach you; for I am gentle and humble, and you shall find rest for your souls; for I give you only light burdens.* (Matt. 11:28–30 TLB).

And yet we tend to disbelieve his invitation. We wonder, *Would God, could God, or even* should *God love me?*

Joy Says, "God Has Plans for Me"

Whether or not God should love us, the truth is that He does. Listen to one of his promises that sounds almost too good to be true: "'For I know the plans I have for you,' declares the LORD, 'plans to prosper you and not to harm you, plans to give you hope and a future'" (Jer. 29:11 NIV). That's good news in a bad-news world.

I suppose the English must have felt this kind of joy when they first heard how the Battle of Waterloo turned out. Ships carried news of the battle to the southern coast of England. From there, signal flags relayed the reports to London. When the account arrived at Winchester, the cathedral's flags began to spell it out: "Wellington defeated . . ." But before the message could be completed, a heavy fog moved in. Gloom filled the hearts of the people as the fragmentary news spread. But when the mists finally began to lift, it became evident that the signals of Winchester Cathedral had really spelled out a triumphant message: "Wellington defeated the enemy!"

Too often we allow our understanding at the moment to color the future. We tend to become so absorbed in our current difficulties that we forget God's promise of a sure, ever-expanding, everlasting future. And because we get so wrapped up in trying to float our own boat or create our own future or fix everyone's problems and meet everyone's needs, we lose the joy of the good news that God wants for us even though we are not necessary.

God wants us! In other words, he appreciates us. William James said, "The deepest principle of human nature is the craving to be appreciated."

The joyful good news is that God loves me and believes I am worth creating a future and a hope for. I am worth saving, I am worth knowing, I am worth prospering—why? Because God says I am. That's good news!

Joy Is Like Good Company

Mark Twain said, "Grief can take care of itself, but to get the full value of joy, we must have somebody to divide it with." How true.

Nothing in life is better than good company, and no one makes better company than God. God is no remote deity, but an ever-present help in time of need. If that's true, then live like it. And laugh like it!

Joy proclaims that God is here and in control of every area of my life. All things in front of me must first appear in front of him. I can *feel* safe because I *am* safe. Jesus called himself the Shepherd of the sheep. So if he is my shepherd and I am one of his sheep, then whatever gets to me must first get through my Shepherd.

Hebrews 11 is often called "the Faith Hall of Fame." It lists the exploits of individuals like Abraham, Sarah, Isaac, Jacob, Joseph, Moses, Joshua, Rahab, Gideon, Samson, and David. At the beginning of the next chapter, we read the reason for the history lesson: "Therefore, since we are surrounded by such a great cloud of witnesses, let us throw off everything that hinders and the sin that so easily entangles, and let us run with perseverance the race marked out for us. Let us fix our eyes on Jesus, the author and perfecter of our faith, who for the joy set before him endured the cross, scorning its shame, and sat down at the right hand of the throne of God" (Heb. 12:1–2 NIV).

As we run our race, we must never forget that we are in good company. Others before us have fought the fight, kept the faith, and joyfully experienced God's goodness and grace.

Joy Comes from Knowing I'm Protected

Read these words that Jesus taught originally in closed session to his inner circle:

As the Father has loved me, so have I loved you. Now remain in my love. If you obey my commands, you will remain in my love, just as I have obeyed my Father's commands and remain in his love. I have told you this so that my joy may be in you and that your joy may be complete. My command is this: Love each other as I have loved you. Greater love has no one than this, that he lay down his life for his friends. You are my friends if you do what I command. I no longer call you servants, because a servant does not know his master's business. Instead, I have called you friends, for everything that I learned from my Father I have made known to you. You did not choose me, but I chose you and appointed you to go and bear fruit— fruit that will last. Then the Father will give you whatever you ask in my name. (John 15:9–16 NIV).

As odd as it may sound, Jesus drew men and women into the kingdom by promising them two things: trouble and joy. The first they had and the second they longed for. But what amazing alchemy is this that he can make even danger and hardship seem joyous?

Jesus understands things about human nature that we grasp only dimly. Few of us feel really challenged by the promise of soft living or by an emphasis on me-first or by a life of easy compromise. We long for the joy of knowing that we're a part of something big, bold, and life-changing.

When I try to pick a moment in my life in which I've felt all these joys at once, I think of a time when I was nine and my big brother was seventeen. Our parents had briefly left us home alone, and I'd been outside playing with some neighborhood buddies. I can't remember what triggered the fight, but I distinctly recall how three twelve-year-olds ganged up on me and whipped me good. I wrestled loose and ran home. I burst through the back door and up the stairs to a room I shared with my brother, crying all the way.

My brother heard me and said, "Come here. What's wrong?" After leveling a few threats, he finally got it out of me. Then, to my utter surprise, my too-grown-up-to-hang-with-his-nine-year-old-brother brother grabbed me by the arm and said, "Let's go." In a flash we bounded down those stairs and strode up the street, looking for those three twelve-year-olds who had beaten me up. I saw them running around the corner of a house. They disappeared around the back and we heard a door slam. Then my big brother—or had he suddenly become Superman?—approached the front of the house and rang the doorbell.

As we waited for those cowards to come out and face us like men, I forgot all about the beating I had just received. I felt great because my big brother took up for me, something that had never before happened. And he was actually *holding my hand* in public! I still remember my chest swelling with pride. I felt invincible. No one dared mess with me now! My strong brother could wipe them all out, one-by-one.

After a long time without getting an answer to his ring, he finally picked up some rocks and started throwing them at the house. *This is cool!* I thought. *I like this!* Eventually the mother of one of the boys shooed us off. As we walked home, I'd never felt so protected, so safe, so secure, so strong. I was with my brother, and all felt right with my little world. After it got dark, my brother rousted me out of the house and again we walked hand in hand, under cover of darkness, looking for the bullies. Though we spent several hours looking for them, we never found them—and I never had any more trouble from them.

I've never forgotten two very important things from that night. One, those twelve-year-olds who seemed so tough the day before somehow shrank that night. Never again did I fear them. Second, my brother got a lot bigger when he came to my defense. He identified with me and even held my hand. I felt ten feet tall in his presence.

The only other person who has made me feel that way is my Savior, Jesus. He makes me feel ten feet tall. Because he has willingly identified with me, I have no need to feel jealous of anyone. He is my provider and sustainer. He promises me a future full of glory, peace, and unspeakable joy.

That's why I choose joy over jealousy. You can, too. It's your call.

PLENTY FOR EVERYONE

Which will you choose, jealousy or joy? If you allow jealousy to hijack your joy, you will constantly feel at risk and victimized by mean, wicked, bad, and nasty people. If you choose joy on the other hand, you will know the thrill that comes from being cured, the rush that comes from hearing good news, the anticipation that comes from knowing the best is yet ahead, and the security that comes from knowing that God's got your back.

Joy knows there is plenty for everyone and believes there's more to winning in life than coming in first. Joy celebrates a world of infinite abundance, while jealousy cowers in a universe of scarcity. Scarcity says, "There's only so much to go around, and I've got to get my piece of the pie. And if you take a bigger piece of the pie, then I must have less."

Plenty or scarcity? Esther Kim made her choice.

The audience at the finals of the Women's Olympic Tae-Kwon-Do competition for the 2000 U.S. Olympic Team Trials in Colorado Springs came for a match and instead got a surprise. Kay Poe and Esther Kim had considered each other best friends since they were seven years old. They had earned the right to face off in the tae-kwon-do finals, but during her semifinal match, Kay dislocated her left kneecap. She could barely stand, and not even her number one world ranking could help her to compete. A win for Esther seemed a foregone conclusion. With Kay badly injured, it appeared Esther had locked up the chance to complete a lifelong quest to travel to the 2000 Olympic Games in Sydney and represent the United States in international competition.

Yet on the day of the scheduled match, Esther Kim shocked the crowd by forfeiting rather than winning by virtue of an unfair competition. By allowing the better tae-kwon-do fighter to represent the United States in Sydney, she won a personal battle over ego and selfishness. And how did she feel about her decision? "Even though I didn't have the gold medal around my neck," Esther said, "for the first time in my life, I felt like a real champion." Esther's generosity of spirit won her the Citizenship Through Sports Award and an all-expenses-paid trip to the 2000 Olympic Games from the International Olympic Committee.

Joy is a choice. And you can make it today by rejecting jealousy.

5

∾

Turning Fear into Faith

One of the great discoveries a man makes, one of his great surprises, is to find he can do what he was afraid he couldn't do.

—HENRY FORD

My father was a simple man who rarely spoke until first spoken to. So when he did speak, I listened.

I still remember one of his favorite pieces of advice: "Son, you can't go through life sitting on the fence." The mental picture of a person sitting on a fence seemed strange to me, because the only kind of fences I'd ever seen were the kind you didn't want to make into a chair. I knew of only three kinds of fences: white picket fences, barbed-wire fences, and electric fences. So I never aspired to fence-sitting.

As I matured, however, I realized that he intended to warn me against fear of taking a risk. He wanted to encourage me to dare greatly. And I've come to understand that "fence-sitting" in the real world not only hurts, it costs. While life seldom rewards indecision, it does often penalize it. In the real world, not to decide is to decide.

It's like the kids' story about Humpty Dumpty: "Humpty Dumpty sat on a wall. Humpty Dumpty had a great fall." I don't wonder how Humpty Dumpty fell. But why was he up there in the first place?

We can apply the fence analogy to many areas of life. For example, when you go to a football game, you notice a fence. On one side stand the players and on the other side sit the spectators. I once heard someone define a football game as twenty-two people in desperate need of rest, being watched by sixty thousand people in desperate need of exercise.

While I love watching great players perform on the football field, I want to be a player, too. It's no fun sitting on the sideline, whether behind a fence or on a wall. In the real game of life, you must choose on which side of the fence you want to live. On one side sit those timid souls who dare not overexert themselves; on the other stand those who come to play, not watch. I don't want to be a fence-sitter or a spectator. I want to be a player. How about you?

WHAT DO YOU FEAR MOST?

One major difference between fence-sitters and go-getters is what they fear most. Some fear failing and looking foolish in the process. Others define failure, not as trying something that doesn't work, but never trying to work out anything at all.

Those who choose faith over fear know it's a dangerous world out there. But they fear most living a meaningless, fruitless life. When I had the opportunity to start a new church with no building, no budget, and only a handful of people, I had to make a fear/faith decision. Would I face up to my fear of leaving the spectator side of the fence by stepping out in faith and trying something that might fail? Or would I fail by not even trying?

I've worked with thousands of individuals from all walks of life, and I've come to believe that the advantages they start out with make no difference. There seem to be only three basic types of people. There are those who watch things happen; we call them spectators. There are those who wonder what's happening; we call them speculators. Then there are those who make things happen; these are the participators.

Participators are the brave-hearted people who see life as an adventure to be lived, rather than a problem to be avoided. Plato said, "We are twice armed if we fight with faith." And Dale Carnegie taught that "the way to defeat fear is to decide on a course of conduct and follow it. Keep so busy and work so hard that you forget about being afraid."

We call fear by many names: worry, tension, anxiety, stress. A recent survey of five hundred people came up with seven thousand fears. But with all the research done on fear, what do we really know about it?

First, it's contagious. You can catch fear from others.

Second, it's limiting. Negative attitudes usually develop in the dark room. Fear is like a rocking chair—it gives you something to do, but it doesn't get you very far.

Third, it's draining. This little four-letter word steals more strength, deflates more dreams, and flogs more futures than any other force in the world. Someone has said, "No passion so effectually robs the mind of all its powers of acting and reasoning as fear."

But the most important thing we know about fear is that God wills us to overcome it, not be overcome by it. Most fears seem to fall under one of two headings: the fear of the unknown or the fear of the unfamiliar.

We Fear the Unknown

The fear in a horror movie arises through the suspense that builds up over not knowing what dangers lurk in the shadows. Alfred Hitchcock said, "There is no fear in a loud noise, only in the anticipation of it."

We go to a haunted house and pay to be scared to death. Elias Canetti, the great Bulgarian psychologist who won a Nobel Prize for his study on the psychology of crowds, said, "There is nothing that man fears more than the touch of the unknown. He wants to see what is reaching toward him, in order to be able to recognize or at least classify it. Man always tends to avoid physical contact with anything strange."

We confront the unknown every day. None of us can predict what a day may bring. Who could have prophesied the catastrophic events of September 11, 2001? Thank God that he doesn't give us the ability to see the future. If we could, no doubt we would die of fright.

From our first day of school to our last day on this planet, we face the unknown. And it is that daily confrontation that drives us to seek the one who knows the future as well as the present and the past. What does God say to us as we face the future? Two words: "trust me."

We Fear the Unfamiliar

My mother once told me something that, as a kid, I thought rather strange. "You can't go swimming until you learn how to swim," she said.

How can you learn to swim until you get into the water? She knew water, of course, but swimming in it was unfamiliar, untried, and untrusted. To my mother, swimming was something to be feared and therefore avoided. But if you apply this same logic to all of life, you'll never drive a car, date a girl, or go to a new place.

Not long ago I spoke with a friend about the amazing tennis I had been watching during the U.S. Open. "I'd love to be able to play tennis," he replied, "but I can't."

Had he ever tried to play? "No." And why not? "Because I never played as a kid," he answered. *So that's the way the adult mind works,* I thought. *It's okay to look silly when you're a kid, but it would never do for an adult to look silly trying to do something new and unfamiliar.*

This philosophy, if applied to everything in life, sounds terrible to me.

In order to stay away from the unknown and unfamiliar, too many of us try to avoid all fear. But a fear-avoidant life is a faith-adverse life: "I don't want to live by my fears, but I don't want to do anything by faith, either. I don't want to have to do something with which I'm unfamiliar. I don't want to have to go into areas where I might fail."

The wrong kind of fear adds up your shortcomings and blinds you to the opportunities. It paralyzes your imagination and disengages your will. Fear can rob you of your self-respect. It is like a bottomless pit or a raging storm in which everything gets swallowed up, never to be heard from again. Fear can multiply your worries and divide your mind—and the Scriptures warn us, "A double-minded man [is] unstable in all he does" (James 1:8 NIV).

I am absolutely sure about two things regarding God and life. First, God loves life and shows it through his boundless creativity. And second, for that reason, I believe God intends life to be an adventure.

Years ago our family moved into a new house built in a new development. In the process of developing the neighborhood, construction workers had to carve out the streets by moving massive amounts of dirt. As they laid out the streets and dug foundations for new homes, they deposited the excess dirt in giant piles at the back of the development. On Saturday mornings, my middle daughter, Lindsey (eleven at the time), and I would spend hours riding our bikes up and down all the hills, around the curves, and through the tall grass. We had a blast and the memories of those times together will enrich me for the rest of my life. We called our Saturday rides "adventure riding"!

I believe "adventure riding" is what God has in mind for you and me. He created you to take an adventure walk with him. Together you will maneuver the hills and curves and hard spots of life. Unlike the bike rides my daughter and I took, however, our Father stays not only with us, but ahead of us and above us. He sees everything coming long before it happens. The power of his omniscience, omnipresence, and omnipotence guides us in a very fearsome world.

Fear Paralyzes Those It Controls

Fear freezes us in place, afraid to attempt anything daring. Franklin Roosevelt, trying to lead America out of the Great Depression, said it this way in his 1933 inaugural speech: "Let me assert my firm belief that the only thing we have to fear is fear itself. Nameless, unreasoning, unjustified terror that paralyzes needed efforts to convert retreat into advance."

Emerson noted, "He has not learned the lesson of life who does not, every day, surmount a fear." What daring, amazing things would you attempt if you knew you couldn't fail?

My father used to work mules. He'd say, "Son, never put two bales of hay in front of the same mule; he'll starve to death." Why would he starve? Because he couldn't make up his mind which bale to eat first. What a graphic illustration of the paralysis of analysis that comes from focusing on fear!

History teaches us that the entire course of the world can hinge on a single event. A small thing done at a critical moment can change the future; we call that a pivotal event. In my father's generation, the pivotal event occurred on December 7, 1941, when the Japanese attacked Pearl Harbor. In my generation, that event happened on September 11, 2001. Everything about the world changed that morning.

Other pivotal events lie yet ahead of us. Although they will vary in significance, the critical choice remains ever the same: Will you recoil in fear or advance in faith?

Todd Beamer chose to advance in faith. He led an uprising against the terrorists who had hijacked United Flight 93 the day other terrorists crashed planes into the World Trade Center and the Pentagon. In a recorded phone conversation with an operator just before he took action, Todd said the Lord's Prayer. When he finished, he urged his fellow passengers forward with a crisp "Let's roll!" In his wife's book about the loss of her husband, she wrote the solemn words, "On September 11, 2001, Todd Beamer completed his time on earth. His life ended while 'daring greatly.' He did not die with 'the cold and timid souls who know neither victory nor defeat.'"[1] We all thank God that Todd and the rest of those heroes of Flight 93 turned their fears into enough faith to take decisive action—especially when the decision would cost them their lives.

Fear Sterilizes Those It Controls

Edmund Burke said, "No passion so effectively robs the mind of all its power of acting and reasoning as fear does." John F. Kennedy said, "The American, by nature, is an optimist. He is experimental, an inventor, a builder who builds best when called upon to build greatly."

God put you on this planet to make a difference. What you do with your life matters. God designed you and equipped you with all you need to live an adventurous life.

But adventures are fearsome things. They require you to turn fear into fruit. Just think of what fear can do to a farmer. Every farmer knows that he must keep tabs on all the forces that could ruin his crops. There could be too much rain or there could be drought. Bugs or blight could attack the crops. A thousand different "what-ifs" must go through his brain each year. Even so, he knows that if he does not borrow the money, buy the seed, hire the laborers, and plant the crops, there certainly will be no harvest.

What is his weapon against fear? Faith! Faith to believe the laws of sowing and reaping that have kept him in business in the past can be trusted again this year. He has to have faith that it will rain and that insecticides can control the bugs. He has to have faith to plan, plant, and plow the crop. If he gives in to fear and plays it safe, harvesttime will be a barren time.

The same laws of sowing and reaping work in your life every day. The Bible warns us that "whoever sows sparingly will also reap sparingly, and whoever sows generously will also reap generously" (2 Cor. 9:6 NIV).

Fear Polarizes Those It Controls

Most of the time it is nothing more than fear that keeps people apart. Liberals fear conservatives. And they each use fear to demonize the other in order to keep supporters on their mailing lists.

Fear lies at the heart of all racism, sexism, and isolationism. Fear lies at the heart of every kind of damning, demonic "ism" anyone ever dreamed up. Who can forget Martin Luther King Jr.'s galvanizing speech "I Have a Dream"?

> I have a dream one day, that this nation will rise up and live out the true meaning of its Constitution. "We hold these truths to be self-evident, that all men are created equal." I have a dream one day, that on the red hills of Georgia, the sons of former slaves and the sons of former slave owners will be able to sit down together at the table of brotherhood. I have a dream that one day my four children will live in a nation where they'll not be judged by the color of their skin but by the content of their character.

The secret to facing your fears is not to tame them, but turn them. We must recognize that fear operates by the law of displacement. Life abhors a vacuum. Fear will continue to plague you until it gets displaced by or replaced with faith.

THE KEY OF FAITH

Faith is as essential to achievement as air is to breathing. Faith unlocks the door to all the blessings and benefits of God. God demands only that He be believed. God doesn't ask for faith; He demands it. He calls for us to trust him before we see results. The quality of your life in the here-and-now rises and falls on your ability and willingness to trust God as your provider and promise-keeper.

Faith makes us proactive. When we see an injustice or an inequity, we want it changed; and where we find darkness, we shine the light of God's love. Jesus taught us to be "salt," not sugar. He called us to a radical lifestyle, not to a radical method that leaves us on the lunatic fringe. He calls us to a life of bold faith. He already showed us that love can change the world—*that* is radical. Other leaders have sought to change the world by force, but Jesus said that all things get changed by faith.

The question is, how does God use faith to change things?

God Uses Faith to Stretch Our Imaginations

The Bible insists that we are to "live by faith, not by sight" (2 Cor. 5:7 NIV). Why? The apostle Paul gave us a powerful reason to have faith when he told the early Christians that God "is able to do immeasurably more than all we ask or imagine" (Eph. 3:20 NIV).

Think of that! I have a big imagination—how about you? I can imagine a lot. But God says, "You imagine it and I'll top it." Most of us came into the world with huge imaginations, but as we grew older, our imaginations began to shrink. By the time we reached adulthood we had been force-fed a steady diet of the things we couldn't do, so as a result of underuse, our imagination shriveled and lost its elasticity. It's hard for some of us to imagine big things because we're programmed to see problems and overlook opportunities.

Lest you consider imagination a childish thing, remember that everything we enjoy today first appeared in the mind of God and only later got transferred into the imagination of a man or woman. The story of Walt Disney World in Florida is a great illustration of this.

Walt Disney died months before the much-anticipated opening of his second theme park. At the opening ceremony, someone said to Roy Disney, Walt's brother, "It's a shame that Walt didn't live to see this."

"Oh, he saw it," Roy replied. "That's why it's here."

God wants to create great things through you and your faith. Only God can see the number of apples in a single seed, but he has given us the power to see, through faith, the possibilities. What faith-inspired dreams and visions are you praying about and planning for right now? Or are you settling for just surviving? Are you just hoping to add to what you have and not lose any more ground?

If all you do is focus on what you don't have or what you don't know or what you haven't done, all you can produce is more of the same. Faith gives the power to imagine, then believe, that you can do it and that you will have the resources to do what needs to be done when it needs to be done. Albert Einstein believed that "imagination is more important than knowledge." Your imagination is like a rubber band—no good until it's stretched. I love what Oliver Wendell Holmes said: "The human mind, once stretched by a new idea, never again returns to its original state."

Are you feeling stretched by anything you're doing? I didn't say stressed; I said *stretched*. There's a big difference!

God Uses Faith to Expand the Possibilities

Thomas Carlyle noted, "Every noble work is at first impossible." When I read about the great men and women of faith in the Bible, I'm blown away by their ability to trust God for the seemingly impossible.

Consider what the Bible says about Abraham's faith: "By faith Abraham, when called to go to a place he would later receive as his inheritance, obeyed and went, even though he did not know where he was going" (Heb. 11:8 NIV). It's hard to pull up roots and leave home— maybe one of the hardest things. It requires saying good-bye to everything familiar and friendly. Yet Abraham did exactly this; and to bump things up a notch, he didn't even know his destination. God said, "Go," and he obeyed. How simple, yet how profound.

My own faith has grown greatest in the face of problems. I've learned that great faith is neither possible nor required in the absence of great problems. If you know how faith works, problems are the best things that ever happened to you. By faith, I've known that the bigger the problem, the greater the possibilities. Adversity harbors the seeds of great advantage. Problems give birth to possibilities. And everything turns on the hinge of faith.

Sir Edmund Hillary became the first guy to reach the summit of Mount Everest. He failed several times. After one of his failures he reportedly shook his fist at the mountain and said, "You have defeated me, but I'll return, and I'll defeat you, because you can't get any bigger, but I can." And he did, in 1953.

If you want to be bigger, better, and bolder, then recognize faith as God's growth hormone. Mark Twain said, "Keep away from people who try to belittle your great ambitions. Small people always do that, but really, really great people make you feel like you can become great, too." Maybe that's why the Bible is so full of ordinary people who did extraordinary things by faith. Faith produced Joseph's moral integrity, Joshua's fearless decisiveness, Esther's selfless courage, Solomon's wisdom, David's optimism, Peter's initiative, and Paul's integrity. We find the key to their genius in the words "Faith is being sure of what we hope for and certain of what we do not see" (Heb. 11:1 NIV).

After all is said and done, the best way to learn about the power of faith is to actually place yourself in a situation that forces you to trust God for big things. My greatest lesson in faith-walking came when I dared to plant a new church. It required not only moving my family to a new city and a new neighborhood where we knew no one, it also required casting the vision for a new church in a city already brimming with churches. But I wanted to attempt something so great for God that it was doomed for failure if God didn't show. I had faith enough that God would be pleased and people blessed by the idea of a church totally grace-based, mission-driven, and people-friendly. I wanted to be part of a church where people could be encouraged to become great, where their dreams and their hopes could be fed, where their burdens could be borne, where their sins could be forgiven, and where their aspirations could find room to grow.

When I look back at what a terrifying thing it was, I wonder how I ever found the courage to attempt such a risky venture, especially with a wife and three children. I realize now that faith gave me the courage. And as I think back, it wasn't much faith—just enough to take the first few steps.

God doesn't require great faith. Jesus promised, "I tell you the truth, if you have faith as small as a mustard seed, you can say to this mountain, 'Move from here to there' and it will move. Nothing will be impossible for you" (Matt. 17:20 NIV).

Still, don't let anyone fool you into thinking that the faith-life is easy. The faint of heart cannot walk by faith. If you dare to do great things, severe and sometimes savage trials will test you. Satan likes to kill things when they're small, when they're just getting started. He knows that if he can kill them at the root, he won't have to worry about the fruit.

But the one thing the devil cannot kill is your faith. The stronger your faith, the greater will grow your power to prevail. Faith will make you courageous and confident at the core, even though the waves rise high and the clouds look black and threatening. Faith is the ability to trust in advance what will make sense only in reverse. It will be your anchor in the storm and the wind in your sails. Faith will thrill you with God's power, sustain you during down times, and contain you during up times.

God Uses Faith to Heal My Body

We know Jesus as "the Great Physician." Wherever he went, he healed the sick. He never walked by a funeral procession without busting it up by raising the dead.

Mark 5 records one of Jesus' most memorable healings. A woman who suffered from severe and chronic hemorrhaging had exhausted all conventional medical methods. She believed that if she could just touch the hem of his garment, she would be healed. By faith, she pursued Jesus, touched him, and got well. When it happened, Jesus turned around and said, "Who touched me?" Everyone denied it. Peter even wondered why he would ask such a question when "so many are crowding against you . . ." But Jesus told him, "No, it was someone who deliberately touched me, for I felt healing power go out from me" (Luke 8:45–46 TLB). Peter couldn't understand what made her different from all the other people touching him. Jesus knew: her faith. She didn't touch him accidentally, but deliberately. Her faith gave her the courage to try and the confidence to succeed in her mission.

A young man in our church, in his mid-thirties, died a few years ago of cancer. At the end of his life, he and his wife asked our elders to come and pray for him in accordance with the words of James: "If any of you be sick, call in the elders and anoint him and the prayer of faith will heal him." We anointed him and prayed.

Two hours later he died.

As I tried to comfort his sweet wife, she said, "You know what? God answered our prayer, because my husband has gotten the ultimate healing." Faith brings a victory that cannot be defeated or denied.

God Uses Faith to Answer My Prayers

The Bible promises, "If you believe, you will receive whatever you ask for in prayer" (Matt. 21:22 NIV). There never has been a prayer of faith that God hasn't answered. Of course, he might say, "No, I have a better way."

A country song popular several years ago carried the title "Thank God for Unanswered Prayers." I've prayed some prayers in the past to which God said, "No." But as I look back, I can only say, "Thank you, God! Oh, what a millstone around my neck that would have been!"

At other times he says, "Grow—you need to be a stronger person. If you continue to grow in faith, great things are going to happen, and when they do, you will need a stronger shoulder."

Sometimes he says, "Slow down—I have a better time." God never wastes the times we wait. Even so, I have to confess that I loathe waiting for anything. I think it's because I grew up in a small town. If we wanted anything good, we had to order it, and it always seemed to take two weeks. Why two weeks, I'll never know, but those weeks felt like months. Sometimes our waiting can feel like that—but we'll never gain anything good by trying to jump ahead of God's schedule.

Finally, at times God says, "Go for it!" He says, "I'm ready to finance the first step, so launch out in faith and go for the gold!"

God Uses Faith to Finance the First Steps

Some people who want to live by faith nevertheless make the big mistake of waiting for God to finance the finish line. But God will never give you all you need to complete your journey in advance. If he did, you would begin to think that you no longer needed Him.

What God will do is give you the go-ahead by financing the first steps. Faith gives us the confidence that what we need to complete the journey will become available on an "as-needed" basis. This not only keeps us from trying to control everything, it also serves as confirmation that we walk along the correct path. God's ongoing provision presents us with signposts along the way to assure us that we remain on the right track.

When God led me and my family to Nashville to plant a new church, for example, I had the conviction that when we bought property for the church, we needed to buy enough for future growth. Too many churches buy too little property while it's still cheap and then try to secure more land later after it becomes prohibitively expensive (or not available at all).

When we finally moved into our first facility after meeting in a school building for ten years, we owned 280 acres. I wonder, *How did we ever afford it?* Then I remember that a journey of a thousand miles starts with the first step. We started by looking, praying, and staying patient. When a parcel of land became available, five of us gave a thousand dollars apiece in order to submit a contract. When we got the contract, we had thirty days to close. Know what we did? We begged and we pleaded during the heat of our summer slump. By the last week of our deadline, we had raised eighty thousand dollars—still woefully short.

While praying in my office (actually the dining room of my apartment), I received a call from a local businessman. "I don't go to your church," he said, "but some of my employees do and they've told me of your dilemma. I've decided to loan you whatever amount you need to get your land." With that phone call, God confirmed that he loves to finance first steps.

God Uses Faith to Achieve His Agenda

Jesus made an amazing promise that I doubt we yet believe or even fully understand: "I tell you the truth, anyone who has faith in me will do what I have been doing. He will do even greater things than these, because I am going to the Father" (John 14:12 NIV).

Imagine that! By faith, we can do even *greater* things than Jesus did while he walked this planet. How? Certainly not by our own power or via our own plans. Solomon warned us that "many are the plans in a man's heart, but it is the LORD's purpose that prevails" (Prov. 19:21 NIV). Faith makes me a player in the great drama of God's redemptive agenda. By faith, I can go where Jesus didn't go and do what even Jesus didn't do. I can be a living, breathing example of what it means to live by faith.

You can make the faith-life believable and accessible to others. They will see the fruit of your life with God and want to know more. This "wanting to know more" becomes my life mission. God's agenda has become my agenda. You can always identify God's agenda because of the "re" words he uses. God loves words like *re*scue, *re*new, *re*birth, *re*ward, *re*claim, *re*deem, *re*store, *re*joice, and *re*fuge. Conversely, you can recognize Satan's agenda by his favorite "d" words. He expresses his work in words like *de*press, *de*stroy, *de*spair, *d*isappoint, *de*fame, *d*isable, and *de*moralize.

God Uses Faith to Reward Boldness

George Bernard Shaw said, "I'm sick of reasonable people. They say all the reasons for being lazy and doing nothing."

God not only rewards boldness; I believe he favors it. Not foolishness, but boldness. God rewards audacious things. I love what the Greek philosopher Seneca said: "It's not because things are difficult that we do not dare. It is because we do not dare that things are difficult."

The apostle Paul warned us, "Let us not become weary in doing good, for at the proper time we will reap a harvest if we do not give up" (Gal. 6:9 NIV). Jesus promised, "You haven't given anything, done anything, prayed anything, served anything in my name that you won't be rewarded for in this life and the life to come." What confident people we can become by investing our lives in bold faith agendas! John Scully, former top executive of Pepsico and Apple Computers, said, "People who take risks are the people you'll lose against."

God Uses Faith to Make You Victorious

"Everyone born of God overcomes the world," writes the apostle John. "This is the victory that has overcome the world, even our faith" (1 John 5:4 NIV).

When you were born, you had no kneecaps. In fact, we don't develop kneecaps until we're three or four. But look at you now! When you were born, you didn't know your name, you had no teeth, no hair, and you couldn't even go to the bathroom by yourself. But look at you now! Already you have overcome so much to be where you are today, reading this book, wanting to build your faith. You are stronger, and better, and more amazing than anything you could imagine.

So stop condemning yourself! Start believing in the God who believes in how amazing you can become! But remember this: he uses adversity to get you there.

God Uses Faith to Assassinate Your Assumptions

Several years ago my wife gave me a beautiful little plaque with this Scripture on it: "Call to me and I will answer you and tell you great and unsearchable things you do not know" (Jer. 33:3 NIV). This is such a powerful promise to me that it hangs by my office door so I can see it every day.

I need to be reminded not to shrink God or try to box him in by thinking I know what he can do or is willing to do. Be cautious with your assumptions and careful with what you think you know about God. I have discovered that even after God has given me a great victory by faith, I quickly forget and slide back into old assumptions and fears about God. I grow forgetful and then I become fretful. Yet David said:

> Do not fret because of evil men or be envious of those who do wrong;
> for like the grass they will soon wither, like green plants they will soon
> die away. Trust in the LORD and do good; dwell in the land and enjoy
> safe pasture. Delight yourself in the LORD and he will give you the
> desires of your heart. Commit your way to the LORD; trust in him
> and he will do this: He will make your righteousness shine like the
> dawn, the justice of your cause like the noonday sun. Be still before
> the LORD and wait patiently for him; do not fret when men succeed
> in their ways, when they carry out their wicked schemes.
> (Ps. 37:1–7 NIV)

Have you ever been to a circus and seen the elephants? Workers chain them to itty-bitty metal stakes. Now, elephants weigh ten tons, so they could easily snap their stakes like toothpicks. Do you know what the workers do? Elephant babies weigh only two or three hundred pounds; that's when their trainers chain them to these stakes. The baby elephants start pulling their chains and discover they can't get away. So their memory banks basically say, "Don't pull on the chain."

We humans sometimes mimic these elephants. Someone tells us when we're young, "You're not very handsome," "You're not very pretty," or "You're not a very good leader," and ZAP!—a mental stake gets pounded into our minds. Often, as adults, we still hang back because of some inaccurate, one-sentence stake driven into our minds years earlier.

Maybe you have been living on the spectators' side of the fence. Your mind says, "Don't pull on the chain. You can't do it." Let God give you the faith to blow away your assumptions and to build your dreams!

THE NEVER-ENDING ADVENTURE

John R. Mott, the great missionary statesman, gave great and godly advice when he said, "Challenge the assumptions with which you are asked to work. If a careful study convinces you they are correct, follow them faithfully. If, however, you are convinced they are wrong, try either to revise them, or abandon them. Do not repeat proven errors!"

The faith adventure never ends. The voyage you just finished qualifies you for the one to come. Charles Schwab said, "A man can succeed at almost anything for which he has unlimited enthusiasm." Edward Teller suggested that "when you get to the end of all the light you know and it's time to step into the darkness of the unknown, faith is knowing that one of two things shall happen: either you will be given something solid to stand on, or you will be taught how to fly."

A life characterized by faith or a life paralyzed by fear—which will you choose? And remember, it *is* a choice. Are you advancing in faith against the unknown and the unfamiliar? Or are you retreating in fear? Fear will make you fretful, or faith will make you fruitful. Choose today to turn your fear into faith, for God promises great reward for those who do.

6

Turning Dreads into Dreams

Lord, grant that I may always desire more than I can accomplish.

—MICHELANGELO

Imagination is a wonderful thing. It can turn a broom handle into a galloping horse, a towel into a cape, and an average day into adventure. With it you can visit far-off places without a plane or a passport. You can use it anytime, under any condition, and without regard to money or manpower.

So let's imagine for a moment that you are standing in the presidential suite in one of the finest hotels in the country. You're dressing for a grand event. Your clothes fit perfectly, every hair seems to be in place, and you have the perfect tan. You've reached your ideal weight and you've never felt better. As you glance in the mirror one last time, a little smile of satisfaction forms—even you have to admit that you feel and look better than most people half your age.

You hear a gentle knock at your door and greet your chauffeur for the evening. He ushers you down a private elevator and into your personal limousine. After a short drive, the limo stops in front of a gleaming, elegant high-rise. You step out of the car and onto a red carpet that leads into the expansive lobby. As you enter, all eyes turn toward you. You can hear the polite whispers and see the discreet finger pointing out of the corner of your eye. The glass elevator whisks you to the top with breathtaking speed. The doors open and as you exit the maître d' greets you and throws open the brass-hinged, wood-paneled doors that open to a magnificent ballroom. As you enter, you see hundreds of other well-dressed people standing to their feet applauding your arrival. Your attention snaps to the right side of the room, at which you not only see the head table, but above it a huge banner that reads, "Happy 100th Birthday."

You're a century old! All the significant people of your life have gathered to celebrate your impact on them. And now I want you to consider a question in real time: Who do you want to be and for what do you want to be remembered? Do you want a parade of people to admit that they didn't really know you, that you were kind of quiet and didn't have much to say, but that you were nice, neat, and never had a bad word to say about anyone? Or would you rather have a long line of friends and family walk across that stage, fighting back the tears, and one-by-one reveal the ways in which God used you to change their lives?

You're acting out and achieving right now, at this moment, the way you'll be remembered later. That you are reading a book about the power to prevail against all odds says a lot about what you want for yourself. So ask yourself a question: If I stay the course I'm on right now, if I continue to think the way I'm thinking, do what I'm doing, give as I've been giving, and try what I've been trying, will I end up where I've dreamed of being one day? If I continue to spend the currency of my influence the way I am now, will I be glad and grateful when I'm at the end of my life looking back?

In other words, if you continue the way you are today, will you arrive at your preferred destination? Do you even know what that destination is? If you answer, "I'm not sure," then now is the time to start making changes.

THE POWER TO ENVISION
A PREFERRED FUTURE

God has given you the power to change the course of your life at any moment by choosing your attitude, changing your aptitude, and taking control of your actions.

You have the power right now to envision a preferred future. But you must want it badly enough to assume personal responsibility for taking control. You begin this process by making a decision that will change everything about your life, as well as the lives of all those whom your life will touch. Make the choice that from this moment on, your life will move onward and upward on the shoulders of your dreams. William James said it well:

> Compared to what we ought to be, we are only half awake. We are making use of only a small part of our physical and mental resources. Stating the thing broadly, the human individual thus lives far within his limits. He possesses power of various sorts which he habitually fails to use.[1]

Dreams are incredibly powerful. They become the culture and context of our lives. It is hard to overestimate their impact on what we can become. The Bible puts it this way: "Hope deferred makes the heart sick; but when dreams come true at last, there is life and joy" (Prov. 13:12 TLB). To ignore our dreams is to invite dreads to hijack our hopes.

All of us have dreads. We face them every day. But the people who make their lives something worth celebrating turn ordinary dreads into extraordinary dreams. If it were easy to do, more people would be doing it.

The power to prevail gives you the guts it takes to leave your rut to follow a different path. And the trip starts when you face up to the power your dreads can exercise over you. Simply put, it's your choice whether you will be drowned by your dreads, driven by your schemes, or drawn into the future by your dreams.

Drowned in Dreads

Carl Sandburg rightly said, "Nothing happens unless first a dream." Which are you nursing right now, your dreams or your dreads?

ly introduce themselves with the word *someday.* As in,
do it, *someday.*" And when the things we pray would hap-
actually happen, our dreads threaten to drown us in a
hat-ifs" or "if onlys."

us whine about work until we no longer have a job. And isn't
it ironic that we pray for children, until we get them? Some people who
pray, "Oh, God, I need to be married!" get married and then cry, "Oh,
what was I thinking?" If we're not careful, we end up becoming a little
pile of nerves and worries and dreads.

What happens when you focus on the things you dread? Job confessed, "What I feared has come upon me; what I dreaded has happened
to me" (Job 3:25 NIV). You can create your own chaos by talking yourself into it.

In college I took a lifesaving course. To pass the course, I had to do
the survival float for a specific length of time. I learned how to do the
survival float well enough to pass, but that's not how I want to live.
"Doing life" by the survival-float method means you try to keep your
nose above the waves of everyday dreads.

Native Americans have a wonderful saying: "When you were born,
you cried, and the world rejoiced. Live your life in such a manner that
when you die, the world cries, and you rejoice." Remember, only dead
things float downstream.

Driven by Schemes

Several years ago I took my family to visit Universal Studios in California. We rode a train around several locations where they filmed
actual movies. On the tour we saw the houses where all the popular TV
shows were filmed. We saw the houses from *Leave It to Beaver* and
Empty Nest. I felt so impressed to see in person the houses I'd watched so
many times on television.

But I got a rude awakening when we turned the corner and saw the
same houses from the rear. These houses aren't real at all. They are just
sticks of wood, propping up a beautiful facade. And that's what schemes
are: beautiful facades without foundation or substance.

T. S. Eliot wisely said, "The last temptation is the greatest treason: to
do the right deed for the wrong reason." You can't always easily spot a

schemer, because they do a lot of the right things for the wrong reasons. They pretend to be a friend, but they really want to use you to get stuff and status. They are big into titles, trophies, and tributes.

In contrast, dreams revolve around love, sacrifice, and significance. They always concern how people can be found, loved, celebrated, healed, encouraged, redeemed, blessed, and benefited. Simply put, schemes are for self, while dreams are for others.

BE DRAWN INTO THE FUTURE BY YOUR DREAMS

Real dreams come from God. He could give us nightmares, but he gives us dreams.

In the book of Jeremiah, God dares us to "call to me and I will answer you and tell you great and unsearchable things you do not know" (Jer. 33:3 NIV). He promises to show you great things! Not miserable things, but mighty things. And he commands us to "forget the former things; do not dwell on the past" (Isa. 43:18 NIV). God says, "Every great thing I've done in the past will pale in comparison to what I'm going to do in the future."

In Isaiah 43, God promises to make a way in the desert. Now, of what is the desert largely made? Sand. So what's the big deal about sand? I'll tell you. Some dreamer found a way to turn sand into silicon and turn silicon into a computer. And we all know what an impact computers have made on the world.

God can take the most mundane thing and make of it the most amazing product. But before sand becomes a computer, someone, somewhere, has to dream. J. A. Holmes said, "Never tell anyone it can't be done. God may have been waiting for centuries for somebody ignorant enough of the impossible to do that very thing." Dreams make the ordinary extraordinary and the impossible, possible.

Dolly Parton attended a high school so small that each student was given the opportunity to stand up at graduation and announce his or her plans for the future. When Dolly's turn came, she said, "I'm going to Nashville to become a star." The entire place erupted in laughter; she felt stunned. Later she said, "Somehow that laughter instilled in me an even greater determination to realize my dream. I might have crumbled under the weight of hardships that were to come had it not been for the response of the crowd that day. Sometimes it's funny the way we find inspiration."

T. E. Lawrence, the famous British adventurer, soldier, and author who mobilized the Arab revolt against the Ottoman Empire during World War I, said, "All men dream: but not equally. Those who dream by night in the dusty recesses of their minds wake in the day to find that it was vanity: but the dreamers of the day are dangerous men, for they may act their dream with open eyes, to make that possible. This I did."

Be careful how you dream in the day, because the size of your dreams will determine the size of your life.

Dreams Draw Out Your Creative Intelligence

God created you with an immeasurable amount of creative intelligence. In Psalm 139:14 David says, "Thank you, God, for making me so wonderfully complex!"

Henry J. Taylor rightly noted, "Imagination lit every lamp in this country, produced every article we use, built every church, made every discovery, performed every act of kindness and progress, created more and better things for more people. It is the priceless ingredient of a better day." And Aristotle believed that "the soul never thinks without a picture."

While all men are created equal, creative energy or the lack thereof soon separates them. George Bernard Shaw said, "Imagination is the beginning of creation. You imagine what you desire, you will what you imagine and at last you create what you will." The great philosopher Pascal declared, "Imagination disposes of everything. It creates beauty, justice, and happiness, which is really everything anyway."

Someone has defined the impossible as something nobody can do until somebody does it. Who knows: you might be the very person whom God wants to dream up a new invention, cure, product, or service that will bless hundreds, thousands, or (dare I dream it) millions! Everything that makes our lives great today—from the car you drive, the phone you use, to the great hospitals, churches, and universities—

all started when God allowed someone to see what was yet unseen. Calvin Coolidge got it right when he said, "We do not need more intellectual power, we need more spiritual power. We do not need more things that are seen, we need more of the things that are unseen."

Dreams Pull Out Our Latent Potential

Thomas Edison is credited with saying, "If we did all the things we are capable of doing, we would literally astound ourselves."

God created you with great potential. This is how the Scriptures explain it: "I praise you because I am fearfully and wonderfully made; your works are wonderful, I know that full well" (Ps. 139:14 NIV). Woodrow Wilson said, "We grow great by dreams. All big men are dreamers. They see things in the soft haze of a spring day, or in the red fire on a long winter's evening. Some of us let these great dreams die, but others nourish and protect them; nourish them through bad days until they bring them to the sunshine and light which comes always to those who sincerely hope that their dreams will come true."

Notice what Wilson said. He did not say that all men are dreamers. That wouldn't be true, because most people feed their dreads while they starve their dreams. He said all "big" men are dreamers. Not the kind of dreamers who dream in the night, but who dream boldly in the day! These dreamers live by the commitment that the vision must soon be followed by the venture.

Too many of us live way beneath our potential because nothing we're currently doing calls for the best in us or stirs our God-given imaginations. Does the following describe anyone you know?

There was a very cautious man,
Who never laughed or played.
He never risked, he never tried,
He never sang or prayed.
And when he one day passed away,
His insurance was denied.
For since he never really lived,
They claimed he never died.

Dreams Align You to Your Primary Purpose

Since my name is David, I have made the following my life verse: "For when David had served God's purpose in his own generation, he fell asleep" (Acts 13:36 NIV). I'm proud to share the name David with the king of ancient Israel. I like David because he knew his primary purpose. He was a battler and a giant-killer. When David went out to face Goliath, he bent down to pick up six smooth stones. He used one to slay Goliath and the rest to go after Goliath's five brothers.

But for all the great battles David fought and won, he really wanted to build a temple for God. But God said, "No, that is not your job. You are not a builder. You're a battler." I imagine that David pouted and became upset. And you know what? God said, "No, no, no. I'm going to give you a builder, as a son." The builder's name was Solomon.

Dreams help you to focus your energy. Let's face it, you have only so much energy and so much time in every day. If you try to do everything, then you will end up doing nothing well. You need to claim a few things as your own. Do those things with all the love you can, as much as you can, as best as you can, and for as long as you can. Knowing God's dream for you helps you do that. Dreams lead to purpose, and purpose allows you to figure out what matters to you. Focus on that and let the rest of life just float by.

Dreams Compel You to Excel

Legendary football coach Vince Lombardi said, "The quality of a person's life is in direct proportion to their commitment to excellence, regardless of their chosen field of endeavor." That's why it is imperative that your dreams come from God. If they do, then you will feel compelled to excel.

Dreams remind you that you're here for something big. Robert Schuller put it this way: "The people who are really failures are the people who set their standards so low, keep the bar at such a safe level, that they never run the risk of failure." Paul said to some of his friends, "As a prisoner for the Lord, then, I urge you to live a life worthy of the calling you have received" (Eph. 4:1 NIV).

A young father was coaching his son's Little League baseball team. As he thought about how to coach the squad, he thought back to how his own coach had such an impact on him when he was his son's age.

"One of the things our coach did was host a picnic for the team at the beginning of the season," he said. "After we ate hot dogs and burgers, he sat us down for a pep talk. He asked, 'How many of you have a dream to one day play in the Major Leagues?' Almost every hand shot up. Every kid with his hand up believed he could do it. You could see it in their eyes. He then told us, 'If that is to happen—that dream begins now!' I was so inspired by that challenge—all of us were—that we practiced and played hard, and we went undefeated for the next few years. All-Star teams from other leagues would play us and lose!"

The man thought that if this kind of motivation worked on him and his teammates, then it might be a good way to motivate his son's team. So he brought all the kids on his team together at the beginning of the season to give them a pep talk—the same one his coach had given him. He asked his team the same question: "How many of you have a dream to one day play in the Major Leagues?"

And not one kid raised his hand. Not one kid believed he could do it. He could see it in their eyes.

"I was speechless," the man said. "The rest of my talk was meaningless, so I said, 'Really? Nobody? Well, go get your gloves and let's throw.' I thought about that day for a long time. What had happened in the twenty-five years since I was a kid? What had come into their lives to steal their dreams? What had convinced them they would never be more than what they were?"

Kids without dreams are like cars without gas or a jet without an engine. Kids must be encouraged, even taught how to dream, because as sure as the sun comes up in the morning, dreams lead to destiny, and destiny is no matter of chance; it is a matter of choice. Destiny is not merely a thing to be attempted, but a thing to be marvelously achieved.

Dreams Give You a Sense of Direction

A famous quote from Thoreau says, "Most people live lives of quiet desperation." In our multichoice, politically correct age, however, the truth might be more accurately expressed, "Most people live lives of endless distraction."

We may go everywhere at once and end up nowhere much, but Jesus lived no such life. Think of how decisive and determined he was when he warned his disciples that he would be rejected by the religious establishment, betrayed by a trusted friend, and illegally accused, arrested, and humiliated. He predicted that he would be beaten, taken outside the city to a garbage dump, and crucified.

"I'm going to die alone," he told them in essence, "but the good news is that after that dark Friday, there will be Sunday. And I'm going to come out of a grave. I want you guys to know, when everyone's calling for me to come down off the cross, you just remember that it's better to come out of a grave than down from a cross."

Sometimes the people who will deter you the most from doing what you were created to do are those who would love you the best. Sometimes the cold water committee is chaired by a parent, a friend, or a sibling. Why? Because everyone, particularly your family, thinks they know what you can't do. They know your name is not "Amazing," but Dud, Doofus, or Gooberboy! They think the closest thing to a superhero you're ever going to get is those Underoos you're wearing.

And let me just say this: don't expect, even if you follow a dream that you believe God has inspired, for everyone to stand up and say, "Man, I applaud that." Some of them will think you're crazy—after all, they thought Jesus was crazy. It is in these moments, in the midst of detractors and protectors, that your dreams will give you what others can't understand or explain: determination. It's required that those who have been given a trust prove faithful.

Dependability means doing what you believe you ought to do, and staying with it. When you know what you're supposed to do with your life, you also know what you need "not" do. A dream relieves you of needing to be "all things to all men." Dreams deliver you from the need to be omnipresent. They are powerful allies, helping you to defeat the people-pleaser inside you. They turn you from a wandering generality into a meaningful specific. The apostle Paul said, "This one thing I do," not "These forty things I dabble at."

I believe Thoreau got it right: "If one advances confidently in the direction of his or her dreams, and endeavors to live the life which he has imagined, he will meet with unexpected success in common hours."

I've lived the truth of the Olympic creed: "The most important thing in the Olympic games is not to win, but to take part." The important thing in life is not to triumph, but to struggle. The essential thing is not to have conquered, but to have fought well. Remember the old Arabian proverb: "An army of sheep led by a lion will defeat an army of lions led by a sheep."

HOW TO FIND YOUR DREAM

Although everybody has dreams, not everyone finds them. How can you find yours? Consider a few suggestions.

Dreams Are Discovered, Not Delivered

As a boy I loved an hour-long television adventure show called *Mission: Impossible.* Each week Mr. Phelps received a secret mission. And each week the secret-mission message ended with the same disclaimer: "If you should get caught, we'll disavow all knowledge of you."

I'm glad God doesn't deliver dreams on tape recorders with self-destructing messages. And aren't we all glad that if we screw up, he doesn't disavow us? As a matter of fact, God invites us to explore and try our hands at new things, because that's how we discover dreams.

I have learned that, at least in the short run, the need is the call. I hear a lot about people looking for their "calling," and while I do believe in the concept of a "calling," it doesn't get delivered to you like an important package from UPS or FedEx. You discover dreams as you go about meeting the needs in front of you.

Jesus illustrated the process like this: "Then these righteous ones will reply, 'Sir, when did we ever see you hungry and feed you? Or thirsty and give you anything to drink? Or a stranger, and help you? Or naked, and clothe you? When did we ever see you sick or in prison, and visit you?' And I, the King, will tell them, 'When you did it to these my brothers you were doing it to me!'" (Matt. 25:37–40 TLB). Every day you run across opportunities to meet needs by serving people. In the act of doing simple things, small things with great love, God allows us to discover the few things he calls us to invest our lives dreaming about and daring to do.

You won't find your dreams in your e-mail folder or your mailbox. Get up, get out, meet life halfway, and see what you discover.

Dreams Are Discovered as You Find a Need and Fill It

What needs around you do you sense are going unmet? What do you see that needs to be done? What things move your heart and grieve your soul? What things get you upset?

For me, it was and is the healthy growth and impact of the American church. I have spent my adult life in a commitment to the church of Jesus Christ. Yet at one and the same time, the church can be the most frustrating thing in the world and the most amazing thing in the world. It is awful when done wrong, and sublime when done right.

Instead of cussing and cursing and being mad at the way it's not, I dreamed about investing my life in trying to make it the way it could be. That was my need; it may not be yours. Theodore Roosevelt noted, "Far and away the best prize that life offers is the chance to work hard at work worth doing."

Find a need and fill it. What is your "work worth doing"?

Dreams Are Discovered as You Find a Hurt and Heal It

Thank God for the sensitive among us. I'm talking about sensitive in the caring sense, not in the "easily offended" sense.

My middle daughter, Lindsey, seems to have a radarlike quality that can recognize the "hurt" in another person. I saw that quality in action when her mother and I attended the summer orientation class for her freshman year in college.

Hundreds of recent high school graduates roamed around a big university campus, looking like the proverbial deer caught in the headlights. As we walked to the football stadium to pick up Lindsey's photo ID, we discovered the desired office was tucked in an out-of-the-way location. When we finally found the place, we got to stand in line for about thirty minutes. On our way back to the university center, way across campus, we passed other kids trying to find the photo ID office. I thought, *Good luck!* But I watched my daughter instinctively identify lost students, go right up to them and say, "You're looking for the photo ID office, aren't you?" They would nod their head "yes," then break into a huge smile of relief when my daughter offered to walk them over to the ID place. I remember thinking, *What is she doing? We're in a hurry! We found the ID place on our own; let them find it on their own. After all, it's getting late and I'm hungry. I didn't take these kids to raise.* My inner voice told me to ditch the kids, but hers told her to help. She saw other kids her age, alone, lost, and intimidated by the whole college experience. Something inside her made her say, "There's a hurt I can heal; there's a person I can help."

Do you want to know how to discover a dream? That's how.

Dreams Are Discovered as You Find a Wrong and Right It

G. K. Chesterton said, "I do not believe in fate that falls on men however they act; but I do believe in fate that falls on them unless they act."

The story of how Jesus cleansed the temple reveals a lot about his character. Mark wrote:

> *When they arrived back to Jerusalem he went to the Temple and began to drive out the merchants and their customers, and knocked over the tables of the moneychangers and the stalls of those selling doves, and stopped everyone from bringing in loads of merchandise. He told them, "It is written in the Scriptures, 'My Temple is to be a place of prayer for all nations,' but you have turned it into a den of robbers."* (Mark 11:15–17 TLB).

It ticked off Jesus that some had turned a place of worship into a shopping center. He let people know of his anger by turning over their tables. Can it be that the Son of God and the Savior of man knew how to show righteous indignation?

Maybe you, too, take it personally when wrong things seem to overshadow right things. Maybe you even tried to express your own righteous indignation, only to find you'd been chastised for it. Now, I agree that misdirected or undirected righteous indignation can become wearisome. But it also may be your soul's energy. When you see things the way they are, you feel more concerned with the way they ought to be. The prospect of how to right a wrong stirs up your creative imagination. It's the way God has wired you, and you need to start thinking about constructive ways to turn your concern into solutions.

Dreams Are Discovered as You Find a Dream and Support It

An admirer once asked the famous orchestra conductor Leonard Bernstein to name the most difficult instrument to play. He responded with quick wit: "Second fiddle. I can get plenty of first violinists, but to find one who plays second violin with as much enthusiasm or second French horn or second flute, now that's a problem. And yet if no one plays second, we have no harmony."

Maybe God is calling you to support the dreamers. Maybe you are like Joshua to Moses, or Jonathan to David, or Barnabas to Paul, or even John the Baptist to Jesus. You could be the one who paves the way for the dreamers to forge ahead. Where would any dreamer in any field of endeavor be without those who support him or her behind the scenes?

During his presidency, Ronald Reagan was quoted as saying, "You can accomplish much if you don't care who gets the credit." I can't think of a better way to find a dream for your own life than to hang around people in the pursuit of God's dream for their lives. Go find a dream and support it. As Paul counseled his followers, "So encourage each other and build each other up" (1 Thess. 5:11 TLB).

IN SEARCH OF RENEGADES

After an assassin killed Bobby Kennedy, Ted Kennedy gave the eulogy at his brother's funeral. Listen to a brief excerpt of how Ted remembered his brother:

My brother need not be idealized or enlarged in death beyond what he was in life. He should be remembered simply as a good and decent man, who saw wrong and tried to right it, saw suffering and tried to heal it, saw war and tried to stop it. And he said, many times, "Some men see things as they are and say 'Why?' I dream things that never were, and say 'Why not?'"

That's the choice you have to make. Will you be remembered as a daring dreamer who refused to accept the status quo (Latin for "the mess we're in")? Or will you miss the opportunity of a lifetime? Will you be a reactionary or a renegade? I vote for the renegade. Renegades never quit, despite the bruises.

In the eighteenth century, Samuel Johnson wrote, "Nothing will ever be attempted if all possible objections must first be overcome." Ask yourself the ultimate question: What's stopping me from living my dreams? Maybe you need to become a little more "unreasonable." Maybe you need to become a renegade.

We need more people who dream up solutions to the problems of the past, present, and future, and fewer people complaining about them. We need more dreamers to become doers. We need more renegades who break conventional wisdom and defy the odds. We need more action and less friction. We need people who can galvanize others with a possibility rather than cause them to be sterilized by fear. We need the medicine of a quality effort more than we need the antiseptic of a mediocre, mild excuse.

When you know you were born to climb, you'll refuse to crawl or coast through life. Don't have it said of you, "When all was said and done, there was more said than done." God "dreamed you into existence," and God implants dreams within you. To pursue your hopes and dreams requires courage, which is the basic orientation of an act of hope. To fail to dream a better future is to deny the God of faithful love, to deny ourselves our own birthright.

If you dare trust God to forgive your past, he will forge an incredible future with you. If you can stop worrying about where you've been, you will enjoy so much more the place you're going. If you will deposit your guilt in the vault of God's grace, you can withdraw the currency of peace and purpose, with interest.

It's time to offer your own solutions to the problems we face. It is time to dream of a better way and then forge ahead to make that way better. It is time to do something great for God and people. We need more God-generated optimism—and you can help to supply it. Remember that no matter how old you are or where you find yourself, when your memories exceed your dreams, life is over for you. Get ready. That 100th birthday bash begins today!

7

Turning Can't
into Can

Never tell anyone it can't be done.
God may have been waiting for centuries for somebody
ignorant enough of the impossible to do that very thing.

—J. A. HOLMES

I count a cheap, two-dollar trophy as one of my most prized possessions. While it has practically no cash value, it marks a huge turning point in my life.

I won the trophy in a local punt, pass, and kick contest. It symbolizes two very important lessons I learned early in life. First, you can achieve more than you think you can. Second, the will to win must follow the will to prepare to win.

Each year our local Ford dealer sponsored the Punt, Pass, and Kick competition. Sign-up always coincided with the unveiling of the new-model cars. While my dad admired the latest-model Thunderbirds, I stood in line to sign up to win a trophy. I only had to pass, punt, and kick a football farther than anyone else—*easy*, I thought, since I was bigger and stronger than the other guys. In the two weeks leading up to the contest, I didn't see any need to train. I figured I could just show up and use brute strength to overpower the competition.

Two weeks passed. I showed up at the local high school football field and performed so poorly that I ranked near the bottom—with scores close to kids half my size. I felt totally humiliated.

This failure, my first really big one, rudely introduced me to my limitations. While losing hurt, I felt greater pain because I knew, deep down, that I didn't deserve to win because I hadn't been willing to train. I resolved to turn things around at the next year's competition.

All by myself, I went into strict training. Every day after school I headed out to the big field in back of our house to pass the ball one way, then walked downfield to pass it the other way. I did the same with punting and kicking. I walked up and down that vacant lot passing, punting, and kicking to myself. I made up my mind to outwork, out-train, and outperform everyone else in my age class. I didn't want a repeat of the past year's humiliation. That painful memory became the fuel for the changes I needed to make.

As the next year's competition drew near, I made a crude countdown chart. I marked off the weeks and days until the day of the competition finally arrived. I was no longer the biggest or the strongest in my new age-group. I looked around at the other guys in line and wondered, *Am I in for a replay of last year's humiliation?* But by the time the last kid had thrown, punted, and kicked the last ball, I had outperformed everyone in my age-group.

I felt the thrill of victory and the personal pride of knowing that I'd worked hard. I'll never forget the sweet moment I heard my name called out over the loudspeaker. I stepped forward and received my prize. In that galvanizing moment I learned that you can do far more than you think you can. Your past does not predict your future as long as you're willing to dedicate yourself to a big goal. Through preparation, you can turn a "can't" into a "can." That moment felt great enough to make me want to do it again and again.

IT'S A MATTER OF FOCUS

A "Peanuts" comic strip illustrates how too many people feel too much of the time. Lucy says to Charlie Brown, "Chuck, you know that life is like a deck chair: some place it so they can see where they are going; some place it so they can see where they have been; and some place it so they can see where they are at present."

"Deck chairs?" Charlie Brown responds. "I can't even get mine unfolded."

I wonder—when did *you* start focusing so much on what you can't do? Can you remember the time and place when you discovered that you couldn't do certain things? Can you remember the days when you liked to draw? Do you remember showing off your artwork to your parents, eager to hear the magic words "That's really good!"? Can you recall those innocent days when you felt unafraid to attempt new things?

For me, I discovered "bad drawing" somewhere around junior high. About that same time, little boys stop wearing bath towels around their necks, pretending to be Superman. We learn early that there are such things as "bad drawings and dumb questions." And we learn to feel really stupid when we become guilty of producing either one.

As we grow to believe in our can'ts, we wake up one day wondering just who we've become. Researchers have discovered that little children laugh more than three hundred times a day. But by the time they reach adulthood, that number drops to less than twenty. I once asked my youngest daughter, Paige, to name her favorite color. She was seven at the time. She thought and then said, "Daddy, my favorite color is red, blue, yellow, orange, green, and black." Her answer hit me like a ton of bricks. She hadn't yet learned that she couldn't have more than one favorite color.

So how do we go from a full-color children's world to a rusty, rutted, routine adult world? A sign on the Alaskan highway reads, "Choose your rut carefully—you'll be in it for the next 200 miles." But can this be what God intended? Is our world supposed to shrink as we grow bigger? Shouldn't growing older make me bolder instead of colder? I've learned that growing older is a privilege, but growing old is a choice.

WHO TOLD YOU, "YOU CAN'T"?

Gordon McKenzie wrote his delightful little book, *Orbiting the Giant Hairball,* after working as the creative director at Hallmark Cards for thirty years. During the early part of his career, he visited elementary schools to teach creative thinking. When he entered a first-grade class, he habitually asked, "How many artists do I have in the room?" Every hand in the room always went up. When he visited the second grade and asked the same question, about 80 percent of the hands shot up. In third grade, the number of self-proclaimed artists dropped to about half. By the time he got to fifth grade, only three or four hands in the entire class reached skyward. And McKenzie asks, "What happens between the first grade and the fifth or sixth grade, that convinces all of us that we are not artists and we can't draw?"

What happens as we grow older? We think we can't draw. We can't speak. We can't do math because our parents had bad math genes and passed them on to us. When people in authority repeatedly tell us, "You can't control your anger, you can't learn, you can't make good grades, you can't write, you can't speak, you can't do anything!" we begin to believe it. And suddenly we become a collection of "can'ts."

By losing the punt, pass, and kick contest, I learned that I could turn "can'ts" into "cans" if I changed the way I felt, thought, and acted. You can, too. By willingly changing the way you feel, think, and act, you take responsibility for the kind of person you're going to become.

So let me ask you: Are you living the life you hoped for and imagined? And if not, why not?

Some folks give a lot of excuses. "I haven't gotten the breaks!" or "I have too many responsibilities!" or "I don't know where to start!" Are you sick and tired of feeling sick and tired? If so, it can change right now. It's your choice!

Any significant change in your life starts with the first choice. So let me challenge you to rethink your definition of the word *can't*. One of my favorite verses in the Bible says, "I can do everything through him who gives me strength" (Phil. 4:13 NIV). This does not mean that I can do anything I want to do, simply by believing in God. It does mean that I can do everything that God calls me to do.

God has never given you a command or a commission for which he has not also given you the power to get it done. I can do everything I'm supposed to do, through Christ. Since all I need to do is what I'm supposed to do, I don't have to do a lot of things; therefore it is fine that I can't do them. It also means that everything I ought to do, and should do, and was created to do, I *can* do—through Christ, who strengthens me.

You Learn by Listening to Your Critics

Turkey-raising experts say that if a turkey gets wounded or has a spot of blood on its feathers, the other turkeys will peck at that spot until they peck the wounded turkey to death.

Can you believe there is an animal so stupid as to keep pecking at the wound of another? I can, because that's what harsh critics do and that is why they cause so much pain.

It's not the big wounds that kill our spirit, but the thousands of little cuts that add up over time. So should we do nothing, have nothing, say nothing, and accomplish nothing in order to avoid criticism? I don't think so, because if you do nothing, achieve nothing, and contribute nothing, you will be labeled a bum.

Face it, you're going to attract critics, and many times your roughest critics can be those closest to you. Remember, in only one place did Jesus Christ not perform miracles: his hometown. People could not see past the boy, Jesus, to believe that the Man could do for them what he had been doing for everyone else. Your critics think they know who you are and what you can do, but all too often familiarity breeds contempt.

King David, one of the greatest heroes in biblical history, certainly found this to be true. He grew up as the youngest of eight brothers. When Israel needed a new king, God sent the priest Samuel to visit David's father, Jesse. Samuel informed Jesse that one of his sons would become the king of Israel. Jesse proceeded to parade his seven oldest boys for Samuel to inspect. One after another they tried to make a good impression, yet one after another God said, "He's not the one."

Samuel finally looked at Jesse and said, "Are these all the sons you have?"

"This is it!" Jesse replied. Then one of the older sons broke in. "Daddy—well, you know there's David."

"Oh yeah, I forgot about him. But it couldn't be him, because he's tending sheep" (1 Sam. 16:11). With that single phrase, "but he's tending sheep," Jesse said it all. David not only brought up the chronological rear in his family, his father considered him the son with the least obvious potential. But in fact, David was the very man God had been looking for. David not only became a great battler and a great king, God called him a man after his own heart.

Be very careful to whom you listen! Your critics can't see the real you. If you listen to your critics, you'll be nothing, have nothing, and enjoy nothing. But worst of all, you might miss the mission for which God has created you. And don't believe that if you could just be a better person, people wouldn't criticize you. You cannot appease your critics, so stop trying to please them. Stop letting them tell you what you can't do, or what you can't be, or what you can't achieve.

Fred Smith, founder of Federal Express, had the idea for his overnight delivery system while studying business at Yale University. He wrote about it in a research paper that received a grade of C. "The concept is interesting," his professor said, "but in order to earn better than a C, the idea must be feasible." Feasible, reasonable, rational—pay no attention to the vocabulary of the little people.

Learn by Living with Comparisons

People compare us to others from the moment we're born. We're weighed, measured, and judged. David certainly illustrates the point.

On one occasion Jesse sent David to take food to his brothers. They, along with the army of Israel, were facing their dreaded enemies, the Philistines. When David arrived, he discovered that no one wanted to go out and fight the Philistines' superwarrior, Goliath. David assessed the situation and decided to volunteer for the job. He reported to King Saul to inform him that he, at least, felt ready to fight.

"Don't be ridiculous!" Saul replied. "How can a kid like you fight with a man like him? You are only a boy, and he has been in the army since he was a boy!"

The Scripture says simply, "But David persisted" (1 Sam. 17:34 TLB).

I like David's response. He didn't accept Saul's assessment. He persisted. Today we would say that David prevailed. He refused to live by someone else's measurement of what he could do. And he found out quickly that "there's not much of a crowd on the extra mile." Most of the crowd lives in the middle, waiting to get a reward for someone else's achievement.

People who pursue excellence make something of their lives. Even though they differ from others, it's not always easy to identify their genius. They live in that rarefied space where the will of God and the heart of man mesh. Because they see themselves as destined for great things, they work hard. They have the will to work long hours, and they feel determined to make the most of their one and only life. How many do you know who sweat it, work hard, take risks? Yet I don't believe that anyone can live the life God intended without making these things a habit.

You Learn by Losing to Your Competitors

From the start, David's family wrote him off. Then he faced sharp ridicule as formidable Goliath compared him to a dog. But by the end of the day, David had Goliath's head—literally.

David knew how to turn his can'ts into cans . . . and yet the going didn't instantly get much easier. In a short while, King Saul—the very guy whose battle David fought and won—considered David his rival, his main competitor. Saul hated David. And it didn't help his temper to hear his own people singing, "Saul has slain his thousands, and David his tens of thousands" (1 Sam. 18:7 NIV). Each time Saul heard the irritating refrain, his competitive nature stirred itself into a rage. David spent years on the run and in hiding, all because the very person whose kingdom he'd saved now saw David as a competitor. David posed no threat to Saul, but no one could convince him otherwise.

Like David, we live in a world defined by winning and losing. We're told, "If I win, you must lose." We tend to bring this competitive attitude into everything. Some people make marriage a contact sport. We haven't learned the advantage of W.W.O.N.D.A. ("win/win, or no deal always"). And so, without a nobler alternative, we settle for listening to our critics, drawing unfair comparisons, and living down the insecurities imposed on us by our supposed competitors.

Be done with listening to the big talk of small people! Stop hanging around with negative people, hoping for a positive outcome. Step out of the critic's corner. As the Scripture says, "I urge you, brothers, to watch out for those who cause divisions and put obstacles in your way that are contrary to the teaching you have learned. Keep away from them. For such people are not serving our Lord Christ, but their own appetites. By smooth talk and flattery they deceive the minds of naive people" (Rom. 16:17–18 NIV).

You have too much important stuff to do to get stuck in the thick of thin things. Get away from gripers who abide no heroes, champion no causes, and acknowledge no accomplishments. Small people attack and belittle others. While Jesus said, "Love thy neighbor as thyself," he also said, "Neither cast ye your pearls before swine" (Matt. 22:39; 7:6 KJV). You need to be smart enough to pick the right neighborhood.

If you get around people who believe enough in you to place great expectations on you, you just might accomplish greatness. I have always prayed, "Lord, let me be the smallest guy in my group. Let me be around people who can stir up my inspirational dissatisfaction and bring out the best in me. I, in turn, want to do that for others."

God did not create you to crown you with mediocrity. He created you and crowned you with *glory*. With glory! You bear his image. God created you and breathed into you. You were born to ascend, to achieve, and to enjoy the adventure.

WHAT CAN YOU DO?

How can you turn can'ts into cans? How can you leave behind the critics and forge ahead into the breathtaking adventure that lies ahead? Allow me to make several suggestions.

You Can Excel at Being You

Contrary to popular opinion, you are responsible only for being the best you that you can be. Certainly God does not expect you to excel at being someone else.

You're not going to stand before God and be held accountable for your brother, or your sister, or your aunt, or the people with whom you work. God made you an original, which means you don't have to live as a carbon copy of anyone else.

But before you excel at anything, you must acknowledge that you have something to offer, someone to please, and someone who gives you permission to live all out. Think about the power of the promise: "The people who know their God shall be strong and do great things" (Dan. 11:32 TLB). Live before an audience of one! God loves you and takes great pleasure in watching your confidence grow. He didn't put you here to please or appease your critics, your competitors, or those who forever make unfair comparisons.

Make it your major preoccupation to be everything you can be. Excel at being you. John Steinbeck said, "It is the nature of man to rise to greatness if greatness is expected of him." But before you excel at anything, you must believe you can. Someone once asked a poet, "If your house was burning and you could save only one thing, what would you save?" The poet answered, "I would save the fire, for without the fire we are nothing."

Feed the fire of your passion to live fully and freely the life God meant you to live. "Show me a thoroughly satisfied man and I will show you a failure," quipped Thomas Edison. Michelangelo said, "If people knew how hard I work to get my mastery, it wouldn't seem so wonderful at all." Spinoza stated, "All things excellent are as difficult as they are rare." Hard is not a bad thing. Everything worth doing is going to be hard long before it gets easy.

The cross has become the symbol of excellence for the Christian gospel. God took a symbol of suffering and shame and transformed it into a symbol of love and sacrifice. He changed the ultimate place of pain, humiliation, and rejection into the place where God at his best offered himself for man at his worst. Can any response to the mystery and majesty of such a love involve no sacrifice, take from me no comfort, or require of me less than the best I have to give? It is the Christian's duty to be faithful, not popular or successful. Willie Mays once said, "Almost anybody can be good at what they do once in a while. It's being good every day that separates the good from the great."

If it bears God's name, it deserves your best.

You Can Derail Your Opposition

I have to make one admission at this point: it's not easy to live a splendid, happy, ever-expanding, always-excelling life. If it were, then everyone would be doing it.

The truth is, it's much easier to live a life of can'ts. You know why? Because it excuses us from suffering, sacrifice, and setbacks. Consider the example once more of King David.

Saul spent years chasing after David to kill him. One night David and his army discovered Saul, unguarded and asleep in a cave. David's commanders urged him to "go in there and kill him! Then you're king and this whole nightmare is over!" David replied, "No. I'm not going to kill him because he is still the king. Besides, I have a better plan. What I've got in mind for Saul will be much worse for him than death."

David then quietly moved about in the cave and a few moments later came out running like a kid who just rang his neighbor's doorbell at midnight. He and his men scurried to the other side of the valley, a safe distance from Saul, and David yelled to his pursuer, "See what I have in my hand? It is the hem of your robe! I cut it off, but I didn't kill you! Doesn't this convince you that I am not trying to harm you and that I have not sinned against you, even though you have been hunting for my life? The Lord will decide between us. Perhaps he will kill you for what you are trying to do to me, but I will never harm you. As that old proverb says, 'Wicked is as wicked does,' but despite your wickedness, I'll not touch you. And who is the king of Israel trying to catch, anyway? Should he spend his time chasing one who is as worthless as a dead dog or a flea? May the Lord judge as to which of us is right and punish whichever one of us is guilty. He is my lawyer and defender, and he will rescue me from your power!" (1 Sam. 24:11–15 TLB).

David didn't mean, "I'm worthless." He simply wanted to say, "You know what? I'm nobody to you, but I'm somebody to God. You don't have to worry about me. God will take will care of you, and God will take care of me. At the end of the day, we'll just let the fruit of our lives stand and defend themselves. And you know what? God's my lawyer and my defender."

He's ours, too, because the New Testament calls Jesus Christ our advocate.

You Can Prevail Against All Odds

God promises his children that "no weapon forged against you will prevail, and you will refute every tongue that accuses you. This is the heritage of the servants of the LORD, and this is their vindication from me" (Isa. 54:17 NIV).

When you place your confidence in God, you can prevail in the face of any opposition or discouragement. Knowing that nothing gets to you until it gets through him should make you bold and unafraid. And if it does get through him to you, he knows that you, in him, can handle it. The Bible says, "The hope of glory is this, God in us!" Not God *and* you, not God *with* you, but God *in* you.

You can do everything you ought to be doing, through him who strengthens you. You can love every person you ought to love. You can do every job you ought to be doing. You can pray every prayer you ought to be praying. You can do everything, as a husband, that you ought to be doing. As a dad, as a worker, you can do it. You can do all the things you ought to do, because God has guaranteed you his power, presence, provision, and providence.

Many times I have found comfort and courage in David's song: "He lifted me out of the pit of despair, out of the mud and the mire. He set my feet on solid ground and steadied me as I walked along" (Ps. 40:2 NLT). And when I am tempted to forget David's counsel, the following poem by Edgar A. Guest gets me fired up:

> Somebody said that it couldn't be done,
> But he with a chuckle replied
> That "maybe it couldn't," but he would be one
> Who wouldn't say so till he tried.
> So he buckled right in with the trace of a grin
> On his face. If he worried, he hid it.
> He started to sing as he tackled the thing
> That couldn't be done, and he did it!
> Somebody scoffed: "Oh, you'll never do that;
> At least no one ever has done it";
> But he took off his coat and took off his hat
> And the first thing he knew he'd begun it.
> With the lift of his chin and a bit of a grin,
> Without any doubting or quiddit,
> He started to sing as he tackled the thing
> That couldn't be done, and he did it.

There are thousands to tell you it cannot be done,
There are thousands to prophesy failure;
There are thousands to point out to you, one by one,
The dangers that wait to assail you.
But just buckle right in with a bit of a grin,
Then take off your coat and go to it;
Just start in to sing as you tackle the thing
That "cannot be done," and you'll do it.

Of course, I know very well that it's one thing to know something and another thing to really know something by experience. When I say that you control your own destiny, I never mean that you are your own God or that you can circumvent God's plans for his world. But I do mean that you can circumvent—or miss altogether—God's will for your life if you don't exercise your power to choose.

You must learn how to control how you feel, think, and act. One must follow the other, because you can't think your way into acting in a manner at odds with how you truly feel. It's not enough to "know" objectively that you can do all things through Christ; you must first feel or believe it in your heart. You win or lose the war in your heart. If God has your heart, your head and hand will soon follow.

Your attitude reveals the condition of your heart. If you have a bad attitude, then something has gone wrong in your heart. Sometimes it's not our critics who get us down or even those who try to compare us unfairly with others. Sometimes, we feel disappointed with God himself. We wonder why he allows others to criticize us, even though they don't know our hearts. Whenever you can't feel the power, presence, and pleasure of God, it's time to stop for an attitude adjustment. If you're sad or mad at God, tell him so. Come clean; be honest; unload—he can take it. Guard your heart through total honesty with God and your attitude will follow.

If you've lost the faith to attempt great things, just remember what I learned through my punt, pass, and kick experience. Your past doesn't predict your future, unless you want it to. God made you to attempt and achieve great things, but you must add the will to prepare to win to the will to win. Helen Keller was right on when she said, "One can never creep when one feels the impulse to roar." Her words remind me of the promise found in Isaiah: "He gives power to the faint, and strengthens the powerless. Even youths will faint and be weary, and the young will fall exhausted; but those who wait for the LORD will renew their strength, they shall mount up with wings like eagles, they shall run and not be weary, they shall walk and not faint" (40:29–31 NRSV).

I pray for you the prayer I offer for myself each day: "Dear Lord, let me attempt to do something so great with my life that I'm doomed for failure unless you're in it." If this prayer reflects your "can-do" philosophy, then respond in the words of an old Chinese proverb: "The person who says it cannot be done should not interrupt the person doing it." Let that person doing the impossible be you.

8

Turning Anxiety into Action

It is in this whole process of meeting and solving problems that life has meaning.

–M. SCOTT PECK

I like to fly—mostly. Other than the hassle of airports themselves, I enjoy most of the flying experience. I can think of only two exceptions.

I admit to feelings of great anxiety whenever the plane hits an air pocket. I don't like those sudden jolts and jerks that make it feel as if some giant hand is giving the plane a karate chop to slam it into the ground.

I also don't care for takeoffs. Just before the plane rises into the air, I sneak a quick look at my fellow passengers to see which ones are trying to look calm and casual. But let's face it—there's nothing "casual" about barreling down a concrete runway at flight-inducing speeds. If the plane doesn't lift off at just the right moment, it quickly runs out of runway. Takeoff occurs at that critical moment when the forces of thrust, drag, and the aerodynamics of the plane combine to lift the craft into the air. When the plane works with the laws of aerodynamics, it lifts off elegantly. When it doesn't, tragedy follows.

Flying and real life have a lot in common. Like flying, life produces anxiety. In both experiences you want the wind beneath your wings to create lift, despite the turbulence and anxiety around you. In both, you have to maintain forward motion. That motion never stops from the time you are born (takeoff) until the day you die (the final landing). Everyone feels anxiety while moving through life's "airspace."

Yet, God commands us to be anxious for nothing: "Do not worry about anything, but in everything by prayer and supplication with thanksgiving let your requests be made known to God" (Phil. 4:6 NRSV). And Solomon warns us, "An anxious heart weighs a man down" (Prov. 12:25 NIV). Excess weight grounds both planes and people.

According to Solomon, anxiety produces excess drag, as in an airplane. Too much drag makes for an aborted takeoff. An airplane faces a kind of drag produced by the mass and shape of the plane fighting against the forces of wind resistance, inertia, and gravity. Except for brief moments of rest, your life stays in constant motion, and yet you can feel the drag that life creates. This drag produces anxiety, and anxiety produces worry. Worry adds weight to your life—not the kind of weight that gives your life substance and structure, but excess bulk and unnecessary baggage. Left unchecked, worry can act like a cancer, attacking both your soul and spirit, and your life can quickly get out of balance. Imbalance serves only to cause more drag, which produces more anxiety, which in turn causes you to add worry upon worry. This chain reaction can quickly form air pockets that jar and toss you to the point that you feel threatened with a crash.

FOUR TYPES OF PEOPLE

Change the image for a moment and think of the grasslands of Africa. Each morning the gazelle wakes up knowing that it must run faster than the swiftest lion, or it will die. But the lion wakes up each morning knowing it must outrun the slowest gazelle, or it will starve. It doesn't matter whether you're the lion or the gazelle; when the sun comes up, you'd better be running.

All of life produces anxiety, whether in the grasslands of Africa or on the runways of modern America. But what fascinates me most are the ways in which we choose to taxi down the runway in an attempt to get airborne. We tend to occupy our personal airspace in one of four ways.

Some People Are Drifters

The people in this group go with the flow. Call them low-trust, low-try people. Because they have found the speed of life and the stress of trying too painful, they've decided to drift along, hoping that something good eventually will happen. They're like driftwood, with no rudder down in the water or sail up in the air.

But I wonder—do they know that only dead things drift downstream? Lifeless objects float with the flow. Everything dead flows downhill, while everything alive struggles to swim upstream.

Drifters don't trust God, and they can't trust anyone else, so they won't try. They don't want to feel anything or desire anything because these activities produce both anxiety and turbulence. So they play it safe by not trying, caring, praying, planning, dreaming, or striving.

But is this what God had in mind when he designed them?

Low-trust, low-try people avoid sources of motivation. If challenged to care deeply or dare greatly, they slink away for fear that it could create motion and movement toward a specific goal.

Recently one organization urged a group of British workers to do nothing to mark the country's second National Slacker Day (a poll suggested that many think they already do little enough). A clothing and record company called Oncus launched National Slacker Day to remind people that life does not revolve around the office and to persuade Britons to stay in bed and relax every February 22.

Yet a survey by My Voice, a polling company, called slacking an ongoing activity. Two-thirds of respondents said they would get as much done and would be more effective if the country switched to a four-day workweek. Almost one-third of those polled said they surfed the Net for an hour or more every day for non-work-related reasons.

Three-quarters of respondents said they used office time for personal e-mail and correspondence, and 59 percent used work time to call family and friends. Among reasons for loafing at work, 13 percent named boredom, 10 percent said they did not have enough work, and 3 percent said they hated their job.

The organizer of Slacker Day was unavailable for comment. A supporter said, "I can't get in touch with him—he probably can't get out of bed."[1]

Carl Sandburg was right: "There is an eagle in me who wants to soar and there is a hippopotamus in me that wants to wallow in the mud." Don't listen to the hippo; it'll get you in trouble. And you will never be happy drifting; God himself will see to that.

Some People Are Drivers

Drivers have a high-try, low-trust orientation to life. We often call them go-getters. They represent the hordes of people who run around from place to place, not necessarily making any progress, but who think they're making great time.

These driven go-getters don't know what they're driving so hard to get, but that doesn't seem to slow them down on their high-speed chase for the elusive pot of gold at the end of the nonexistent rainbow. They're barreling down the runway of life, and God help you if you get in the way!

Drivers are like the metal ball in a pinball machine. They bounce, often violently and unpredictably, off every obstacle they hit. And for them it doesn't matter much who gets dinged along the way. They're out there "making it happen." They have totally bought in to win-lose. For them, the only progress comes at the expense of others. They have no time for people, God, or, sadly enough, even themselves.

The Bible warns about the terrible turbulence that this kind of person can expect to encounter. Solomon said, "I denied myself nothing . . . I refused my heart no pleasure. My heart took delight in all my work, and this was the reward for all my labor. Yet when I surveyed all that my hands had done and what I had toiled to achieve, everything was meaningless, a chasing after the wind; nothing was gained under the sun" (Eccl. 2:10–11 NIV).

A man in a hot-air balloon realized he was lost. He decided to reduce altitude, and as he descended he spotted a woman below. "Excuse me," he said, "can you help? I promised a friend I would meet him an hour ago, but I don't know where I am."

The woman replied, "You are in a hot-air balloon hovering approximately 30 feet above the ground. You are between 40 and 41 degrees north latitude and between 59 and 60 degrees west longitude."

"You must be an engineer," said the balloonist.

"I am," replied the woman. "How did you know?"

"Well," answered the balloonist, "everything you told me is technically correct, but I have no idea what to make of your information and I am still lost. Frankly, you've not been much help so far."

The woman responded, "You must be in management."

"I am," replied the balloonist. "But how did you know?"

"Well," said the woman, "you don't know where you are or where you are going. You have risen to your current position due to a large quantity of hot air. You made a promise that you have no idea how to keep, and you expect people beneath you to solve your problems. The fact is, you are in exactly the same position you were in before we met—but now, somehow, it's my fault!"

The driver's motto is, "I may not know where I am or why I am where I am, but I'm making great time."

Some People Are Dreamers

Dreamers are high-trust, low-try people. Dreamers place their faith in faith itself. They talk a lot about God and dreams—and I have to admit, I have a soft spot in my heart for them. Dreamers come in two very distinct models. Some dreamers dream in the night. They never wake up! The other type dream in the day. They know that a vision must be followed by the venture, or else it amounts to nothing more than fanciful speculation. They believe, but they also act. The Bible asks, "Are there still some among you who hold that 'only believing' is enough? Believing in one God? Well, remember that the demons believe this too—so strongly that they tremble in terror! Fool! When will you ever learn that 'believing' is useless without doing what God wants you to? Faith that does not result in good deeds is not real faith" (James 2:19–20 TLB).

Some People Are Daring-Doers

Doers are the high-trust, high-try people among us. They are our builders, creators, writers, statesmen, and heroes. They have lifted off and occupy their personal airspace with purpose and passion. They know what to do and why they're doing it.

Doers lead high-impact lives because, somewhere along the way, they have discovered the genius of the "and." They try as if it all depends on them, and yet they trust, knowing that it truly all depends, ultimately, on God. Trusting is no good without trying because he who truly trusts, also tries.

You'll never meet a more unlikely group than daring-doers. They're ordinary people who do everyday things with great love. Consider what's happened out of the horrific attacks of September 11, 2001. When the Twin Towers of the World Trade Center burst into flame, who answered the call? Firefighters, police officers, and emergency medical personnel. These individuals are our society's first-responders. They train in obscurity and much of their day-to-day routine looks mundane and trivial. But when the call came for courage and unflinching bravery, they went without pause or hesitation.

What heroes do we celebrate post-9/11? Are they rock stars, movie stars, and one-hit wonders? No—just ordinary men and ordinary women, doing their jobs, in extraordinary moments. The firemen and police who rushed into the Twin Towers and up those stairs didn't say, "It must be God's will that these people perish." They did their jobs. They didn't try to play God, and neither should we. At some point, what you say you are and what you claim to believe will force you to behave as if you really do believe it. During times of change, crisis, and the ensuing discontinuity, the genius of the high-trust, high-try lifestyle comes to the forefront.

TRUST AND TRY

Flying is scary, but it's thrilling, too. I love getting on a plane in Nashville and getting off it in L.A. It's great to fly!

You were created to soar. You are not a turkey, even though you may hang around several (or perhaps you're related to a few). I agree with

Saint Augustine, who said, "God is more anxious to bestow his blessings on us than we are to receive them." In other words, what God wants to do for us, he waits to do through us.

An Old Testament hero named Gideon made this thrilling discovery. We first meet this young nobody during a particularly low moment in Israel's history: "When the angel of the LORD appeared to Gideon, he said, 'The LORD is with you, mighty warrior.' 'But sir,' Gideon replied, 'if the LORD is with us, why has all this happened to us? Where are all his wonders that our fathers told us about when they said, "Did not the LORD bring us up out of Egypt?" But now the LORD has abandoned us and put us into the hand of Midian.' The LORD turned to him and said, 'Go in the strength you have and save Israel out of Midian's hand. Am I not sending you?'" (Judg. 6:12–14 NIV).

Desert nomads called the Midianites and the Amalekites had overrun Israel. These desert warriors used their camels to swoop in, destroy crops, kill and plunder, then disappeared back into the sands with such speed that the Israelites couldn't catch them. The crisis threatened the very existence of the people of God.

And what was God's solution to this dilemma? Gideon, a nobody from the smallest tribe of Israel.

We might describe Gideon as an underachiever, caught in the middle of a war. He felt terrified, and rightly so. Therefore he did what any of us might do: he hid in the bottom of a barn, scrounging for a few scraps of food.

It naturally confused him when the angel of the Lord called him a "mighty warrior." I'm sure he thought, *Mighty what? Mighty warrior? Me?* Gideon seized the opportunity to speak his mind. He responded to the angel with undisguised cynicism: "If this is the Lord with us, I'd hate to see what it'd be like if the Lord wasn't with us."

Have you ever felt that way? *If this is God being good to us, I'm not sure I want him to be any better.* And Gideon had a good argument. He looked around and saw a hard world, a difficult world, a painful world, a world in which good people die. He saw a world in which he couldn't seem to trust anyone or anything. So where was God in all this mess? *I thought we were supposed to be God's chosen people.*

But what a response he received!

"Gideon," said the angel, "it is bad, but here's what I want you to do: go in the strength you have and save your country."

Oh, is that all? R-i-i-i-ight.

I'm sure Gideon did not expect such a declaration. In light of the atrocities he had witnessed, he probably thought, *Strength? I don't have any strength! I am a nothing, a nobody. I'm hiding in this barn precisely because I am not brave, I am not bold, and I have nothing to offer anybody, especially in the face of the overwhelming odds we face. I'm timid, tired, and ticked-off—and the last thing I want to do is die a martyr's death.*

Yet the angel's words stood: "Go in the strength you have and save Israel out of Midian's hand. Am I not sending you?" (Judg. 6:14 NIV). Perhaps Gideon thought, *This must be a gross case of mistaken identity. There is nothing a guy like me can do. I'm powerless and well on my way to feeling helpless and hopeless.*

But again the words of the angel of the Lord came through loud and clear: "Go in the strength you have. . . . Save your country!"

In the story of Gideon we encounter a universal truth: we must be the change we want to see. God doesn't do magic. He does miracles, not magic. God would deliver Israel from her enemies, but he required a daring-doer to lead the way. He called upon Gideon to deliver his country and at the same time to trust God to show up and make it happen.

And happen it did!

Gideon gathered an army of 32,000 men—but God said he gathered too many. God told Gideon to send home all the men who felt afraid. That cut the number down to 3,000. Still too many. God told Gideon to send the remaining men to the water; all the men who lapped up water like dogs were to stay, the rest were to go home. That episode cut the number down to 300. And with these 300 daring-doers, Gideon, following God's specific instructions, removed the Midianite threat. That was how God did it then, and it remains the way he does it today.

As a kid, I loved the story about how Jesus fed the five thousand. When you take into account all the families and extended families, there could have been double or even triple that number. These many thousands listened to Jesus speak all day long. They had to feel tired, hot, and most of all, hungry. The disciples worried about crowd control and asked Jesus to send them away to find food on the way home. Jesus' response sounded like the advice the angel of the Lord gave to Gideon.

He told his disciples to feed the hungry crowd. They objected, "We don't have any food!" But Jesus wouldn't let them off the hook. He told them to look again. When they did, they came up with five loaves of bread and two fish.

And with that small beginning, Jesus fed everyone, with some left over. His disciples learned that day the lesson of Gideon from many centuries before. We must be willing to do our part, no matter how small or seemingly insignificant, before God will do his part. It is not trust *or* try, but trust *and* try.

Have you ever had a similar experience with God? If you haven't, you will. From God's perspective, you never have nothing. You never have no power, no options, no choices. You may face times when you have "nothing much," but all God needs is what you have. Then he says, "Give it to me." And the rest is history.

Maybe God is saying to you today, "Do something!" But you may say, "I have nothing." And he replies, "Nothing? No, you always have something!" What you have may not be enough to get the job done, but it is definitely enough to start.

Remember, you always have the power to choose your attitude, change your aptitude, and control your actions or responses. You control how you feel, think, and act.

THREE HABITS OF ACTION-ORIENTED PEOPLE

Those who occupy their airspace as high-trust, high-try people have an action orientation. They are purposeful people. Anxiety gets them moving. Daring-doers have three habits in common.

They Think Big

Have you ever focused on your problems so much that you can see only problems? If you continue on this track, your problems will expand until they eclipse everything else. And when that happens, you see and feel only pain—the pain of divorce or the pain of separation or the pain of a job lost. If you're not careful, the pain will expand to fill your entire universe.

God says, "You know what? Think big. Think about me." Jesus said, "With God all things are possible" (Matt. 19:26 NIV) and "Nothing is impossible with God" (Luke 1:37 NIV). He promised, "What is impossible with men is possible with God" (Luke 18:27 NIV).

I love the idea of "big thinking" as illustrated in the account of Peter's walk on water. All the disciples in the boat saw Jesus walking on the waves, but only Peter said, "Can I walk on water?" That says two things: that he believed Jesus Christ was big enough to walk on water; and that he believed a relationship with Christ would give him the right to request that he, too, could walk on water.

But even with Jesus calling you out to walk on water, you still have to "think outside the boat." You must be willing to get your feet wet. In other words, what God wants to do *for* you, he waits to do *with* you. Some of us feel stuck with "inside the boat" thinking, because no one has given us permission to think big. When we get serious about trusting God, however, we have to remember that God is the ultimate big thinker! And when we start thinking God's way, the possibilities begin to expand. We start thinking big, dreaming big, and daring big. We think, *I am a doer of dreams. I'm not just a dreamer.*

We have to learn to close the loop between high-trust and high-try. Abraham Lincoln said, "Towering genius disdains a beaten path. It seeks regions hitherto unexplored." And Oliver Wendell Holmes said, "The human mind, once stretched by a new idea, never regains its original dimensions." Peter Senge, the noted author and professor from MIT, said rightly, "In the absence of a great dream, pettiness prevails."

Do you realize how often "the experts" have been proved wrong by those who dare to do great things? In the last century, Lord Kelvin, a physicist and president of Britain's prestigious Royal Society, stated that "radio has no future." He also contended, "Heavier-than-air flying machines are impossible" and "X rays will prove to be a hoax." About the same time, a British parliamentary committee dismissed Thomas Edison's incandescent lamp as "unworthy of attention of practical or scientific men." In 1889 the director of the United States Patent Office urged President William McKinley to close down the office because "everything that can be invented has been invented."

God is into big things like worlds, stars, and galaxies. He does miracles, raises the dead, and brings beauty out of broken things. And he wants us, so far as we are able, to follow his big-dreaming example.

They Act Small

Daring-doers think big, but act small. Humble, action-oriented achievers know that all great journeys to exotic destinations begin with the first small steps.

In life, the real world comes only in versions called "as is." Every time you refuse to do small things, you get smaller. If you're waiting to be amazing when your ship comes in, you're in for a long wait.

Someone told me years ago, "If you are too big for a small thing, you will always be too small for a big thing." The Scriptures put it this way: "Whoever can be trusted with very little can also be trusted with much, and whoever is dishonest with very little will also be dishonest with much. So if you have not been trustworthy in handling worldly wealth, who will trust you with true riches? And if you have not been trustworthy with someone else's property, who will give you property of your own?" (Luke 16:10–12 NIV). The Old Testament warns us that God does not look favorably on the one "who despises the day of small things" (Zech. 4:10 NIV).

Too many of us waste too much of our precious time waiting to do the big thing in the limelight. John Wooden, the legendary basketball coach at UCLA, didn't see it that way. He said, "Do not let what you cannot do interfere with what you can do." Anyone can be daring right now in this moment, because anyone can begin. Do *something,* no matter how small and insignificant it may seem.

A novelist went to work on his latest book at his beach house. He rose very early each morning to walk on the beach before getting started. One day he encountered an elderly man on the beach. The man walked with a cane, carefully surveying the beach left exposed by the receding tide. Every now and then he bent to pick something up and toss it into the ocean. The novelist watched with fascination as the man carefully scanned the beach before him. The writer finally realized that the man was looking for starfish. Every time he saw one lying helpless in the sand, unable to get back to the ocean on its own, he would lovingly pick it up and toss it gently back into the sea. The novelist approached the old man and asked him why he was doing this.

"The starfish are left behind after the tide goes out," the old man said. "If they don't get back into the ocean they will dry up and die beneath the hot summer sun."

"But there are endless miles of beach and there must be millions of starfish," the novelist said. "Surely you don't think you can save them all. What difference can your efforts possibly make?"

Slowly the old man bent over and picked up another starfish. As he tossed it into the ocean he said, "It makes a difference to that one."

They Lean Hard

My wife, Paula, and I keep a list of things we want to do. One such thing was to ride the waves on a big sailboat.

Not long ago, while on a trip to Key West, Florida, we boarded a big sailboat, a double schooner. A double schooner has two masts and a sizable crew, so as passengers, we weren't helping much. We had come to observe, or so we thought, until the sails caught a big gust of wind.

At that moment the captain called us to the opposite side of the boat and screamed out for everyone to lean hard. I found myself leaning out over the boat, thinking that if the wind died down suddenly, I'd pitch overboard. Then we heard the captain's reassurance: "Lean hard into the wind. Trust the wind, folks; it'll carry us all home if we lean hard into it."

In the same way, trust God for big things. Lean hard into him with your full weight. He can be trusted to carry you home.

FINDING STRAIGHT PATHS

Liftoffs can bring moments both anxious and exhilarating. Think back to the last time you found yourself rushing to the end of the runway, strapped to a seat bolted to the floor of a giant, trembling, metallic cylinder—and then in a moment of high anxiety, it successfully lifted off. Hot diggity!

At all moments of liftoff, God says to us, "Open your heart, give me all you've got, and lean hard into me." Solomon gave us the great prom-ise: "Trust in the LORD with all your heart, and do not rely on your own insight. In all your ways acknowledge him, and he will make straight your paths" (Prov. 3:5–6 NRSV). And Saint Francis de Sales gave his own testimony: "The same everlasting Father who cares for you today will take care of you tomorrow and every day. Either he will shield you from suffering, or he will give you strength to bear it. Be at peace, then, and put aside all anxious thoughts and imaginations."

When you have done all that you can and feel out of breath, it is a sweet thing to suddenly feel the breath of God and the wind beneath your wings. In that newfound strength, you can take action . . . and leave anxiety on the tarmac far below.

9

Turning Stress into Strength

There are no shortcuts to any place worth going.

—BEVERLY SILLS

In the last chapter I mentioned how I keep a list of things I want to do before I'm done. Running a long-distance race used to be on that list; I checked it off in college after finishing a 10K race.

For ten months I trained each day. Over time I began to take an interest in things that never mattered much to me in my more sedentary days. Things like running shoes, running clothes, and running magazines began to pique my interest. I began to choose more carefully the foods I ate. I learned about carbohydrate-loading on the one hand, and protein shakes on the other. As the months passed, I felt my body responding to the demands I was making of it. Runners call this the training effect. The training effect comes from pushing yourself just far enough so that your body must change to respond to the new demands, but not so far that the stress and strain cause your body to break down and injure itself.

On race day, thousands of athletes showed up to run. It quickly became clear who had taken the race seriously and who hadn't. Those who trained diligently stood out from those who just showed up.

As I've thought back about that experience, I realize that life itself is a lot like preparing to run a race (maybe that's why we're called the human race). Every race features a balancing act between enough stress to achieve the training effect and too much stress, which results in injury. That delicate balance makes the difference between living on the razor's edge or achieving the racer's edge.

Every winner looks for a winning edge. Even the Scriptures use a racing analogy to teach us about running in the human race. The apostle Paul said, "Press on toward the goal to win the prize" (Phil. 3:14 NIV). God created us to be winners, not whiners. And doing life God's way gives us the training effect. I need to run my race with guts and grace, but I also need major amounts of help.

STP: THE RACER'S EDGE

In high school, I landed a spot on a local drag-racing team. My first assignment: help build an engine from the ground up. I had to coat all the engine parts with a lubricant called STP, a miracle product that used the slogan "STP, the racer's edge."

As we built the engine, we coated every movable part. None of its metal parts could ever touch one another without a lubricant between them. STP adheres to the surface and serves as a protective coating to fight an engine's two worst enemies: heat and friction.

Heat and friction not only damage moving parts; they also produce stress for people in motion. Therefore, God has graciously built a type of STP into our personal makeup: *S*elf-control, *T*raining, and *P*erseverance. The acronym helps me to think about what I must do each day to prepare myself for the race ahead. And because our race is more like a marathon than a hundred-yard dash, we all need to protect against heat and friction.

Most historians consider the apostle Paul to be the greatest Christian missionary who ever lived. He almost single-handedly Christianized the known world—and he had to walk most of the way. Think of that! No cars, no Internet, no phone, no planes. You put on your sandals; you walk to town; you talk; and then you walk to the next town.

Paul graciously pulled back the curtain to let us in on the inner workings of his life. He revealed his secrets to turning ordinary stresses into extraordinary strengths, using the STP formula: self-control in the defining moments; training in the idle moments; and perseverance in the low moments.

Self-Control in the Defining Moments

Paul says, "In a race, everyone runs but only one person gets first prize. So run your race to win. To win the contest you must deny yourselves many things that would keep you from doing your best. An athlete goes to all this trouble just to win a blue ribbon or a silver cup, but we do it for a heavenly reward that never disappears" (1 Cor. 9:24–25 TLB).

When I started training for my race, I had to start telling my mind and emotions what I wanted them to do. I had to bring discipline into my life. I had to do it for myself, because my wife couldn't do it for me. Unlike most of the things I had done to that point, I didn't have to run to get a passing grade or a winner's cup. I felt a self-imposed, inner compulsion rather than any external pressure.

Self-control means that I put limits on my freedom. I remained totally free not to run at the end of a long, hard day, but such a choice meant that I chose not to run in the race for which I had already registered. Paul put self-control in perspective like this: "I can do anything I want to if Christ has not said no, but some of these things aren't good for me. Even if I am allowed to do them, I'll refuse to if I think they might get such a grip on me that I can't easily stop when I want to" (1 Cor. 6:12 TLB).

Winners know that playing conditions are rarely perfect. They know how to play hurt. They line up and move through the pain. Too many stop at the pain and never push through to know the surge of energy that comes beyond the pain. Doing the right thing, the smart thing, the best thing before you have to brings major victories over the stresses of life that otherwise leave you drained and worn out. The high-octane engine of self-control gives you the inner strength to will yourself to do whatever must be done.

If you want self-respect, then you must develop self-control. My self-image is a product of my self-worth, and my self-control is a product of my self-image. So in order to develop self-respect, I must exercise self-control in keeping with my self-image, which is determined by who God says I am. Since God says I am loved and strong, I must act in sync with what God says I am in order to feel the way God says I should.

Deny yourself the very thing you want and eventually you will have more of it. Yet denying yourself what you want seems foreign in this age of quick and easy. If ideas like self-denial and self-discipline don't appeal to you, consider this: if you don't exercise control and discipline for yourself, then someone else will do it for you.

I taught my children that because I love them, they could expect that I would discipline them in the privacy of our home so they wouldn't face the embarrassment of being disciplined by society in public. We discipline those who step outside certain boundaries; we call them laws. We don't discipline lawbreakers because we love them, but because we fear them. We put them in jail, not for their protection, but for ours!

At the other end of the spectrum we have men and women who don't need laws. Do you know why? Because they don't live on the edge of life. They live at the very center. They demand more of themselves. They never ask, "What can I do to just get by?" These people run their race to win. They are not into minimum requirements, but maximum performance.

God has created you to be free, he will not force you to do certain things. He has given you a billion-dollar body and a trillion-dollar brain, but he will not force you to use either one of them. If you want to fritter away your life, worrying and wringing your hands and seeking a comfortable place, go ahead and pursue it. But if you want to squeeze the absolute most out of every day, you must develop self-control.

There is so much more inside you than anyone can observe from the outside. Appearances truly deceive. But the "real you" will never come out until you demand more of yourself. You cannot earn God's love, but you must earn your own. When some people hear someone say, "God loves you," it doesn't ring true, because they don't like or love themselves very much. They wonder, *How could the God who knows me completely ever love me totally?*

Self-respect comes from self-control. You can get by with doing a lot of things, but you can't do them and gain any sense of self-respect. If you follow your feelings, you'll more than likely follow them down the path of least resistance. I've heard men say, "I'm going to leave my wife because I just don't *feel* that I love her." I've counseled others who lament, "I'm going to quit my job because I just don't *feel* that it's fun anymore." When someone gets to that place of "giving up," it is hard to get them to understand that they will never feel the way they want to feel until or unless they start doing what they ought to do. When we do what we ought to do, eventually we will feel the way we want to feel. But it takes the strength of self-control to impose a moral imperative upon yourself.

Remember, self-control is about making choices before you have to. And when you impose self-control, you can expect to experience the training effect.

Training in the Idle Moments

A sign on the wall of my daughter's gymnastics class made such an impact on me that I still remember its message many years after first reading it: "If you want to perform like a champion, you must practice like one!"

The Bible teaches the same thing, using a boxing metaphor: "So I run straight to the goal with purpose in every step. I fight to win. I'm not just shadow-boxing or playing around. Like an athlete I punish my body, treating it roughly, training it to do what it should, not what it wants to" (1 Cor. 9:26–27 TLB).

You lose no time by taking the time to prepare. If you ever feel tempted to cut your life training short, remember, "Everyone pays the price, but not everyone pays the same." The athlete pays the price when he or she gets out of bed and hits the track while others remain tucked away in bed. The athlete who hopes to win knows that he must pay the price up front, ahead of time. While others enjoy a snack, he's out on the track. While others go to the movies, he's out running the extra mile.

Great musicians pay the price by practicing their scales. Strong performers know that genius is forged in private before it is displayed in public. Greatness in the concert hall follows hours of labor in the practice room. Great athletes are made not on the playing field, but on the practice field. The game gets decided not in the homecoming game in front of a cheering crowd, but in the summer solitude of two-a-days and torturous pain.

I love what Ignacy Paderewski, the great Polish pianist, statesman, politician, and composer, said, just before his death in 1941. "If I don't practice one day, I know it," he said. "If I don't practice the next day, the orchestra knows it. If I don't practice the third day, everyone knows it."

Do you have that kind of attitude? Do you demand more *of* yourself because you demand more *for* yourself?

When I put myself on a training schedule, things changed dramatically. Starting out, I trained at the high school close to where we lived. It had an artificial track, shaped in an oval—flat with a nice, smooth surface. At first, I could hardly get around the thing one time without feeling as though I were about to have a heart attack. But after three or four weeks, I could trot around for one complete mile without stopping. I was amazed at how quickly I began to feel the training effect. How wonderful God has made you and me! He has made our physical, emotional, and spiritual makeup so that we can adapt to the demands of stress and strain by developing strength and endurance.

Several years ago my wife asked me to plant flowers around our new house. Since I had never done such work before, I didn't think to wear gloves, and by midmorning I had developed several blisters. By late afternoon, my hands began to bleed. "Honey," I said, "my hands are bleeding."

"Well," she replied, "put on some gloves and go back out there and be a man."

You know what? The next day those blisters began to scab over, and before long my hands had developed calluses. But at first I kept telling my wife, "Honey, if I keep getting blisters at this rate, by tomorrow morning, I'll have nubs. I'll actually wear away my hands if I keep this up." Hogwash! God has so fearfully and wonderfully made us that if our work gives us blisters, God will give us calluses. Under managed stress, our bodies respond to the demands made of them. And that's true not only physically, but emotionally and intellectually as well. We call this amazing, glorious phenomenon the training effect. Paul describes it this way:

> Not that I have already obtained all this, or have already been made perfect, but I press on to take hold of that for which Christ Jesus took hold of me. Brothers, I do not consider myself yet to have taken hold of it. But one thing I do: Forgetting what is behind and straining toward what is ahead, I press on toward the goal to win the prize for which God has called me heavenward in Christ Jesus. All of us who are mature should take such a view of things. And if on some point you think differently, that too God will make clear to you. (Phil. 3:12–15 NIV).

Perseverance in the Low Moments

Shakespeare said, "There is a tide in the affairs of men which taken at its flood carries onto fortune. Omit it and all of life's journeys are bound for the shallows." Believe it or not, it's the overwhelming circumstances in life that God uses to carry us to our greatest effectiveness. If we fail to prevail at those low moments, we will have no high ones to celebrate.

Paul expressed his own concern like this: "I fear that after enlisting others for the race, I myself might be declared unfit and ordered to stand aside" (1 Cor. 9:27 TLB). In the book of Hebrews we read,

> *Since we have such a huge crowd of men of faith watching us from the grandstands, let us strip off anything that slows us down or holds us back, and especially those sins that wrap themselves so tightly around our feet and trip us up; and let us run with patience the particular race that God has set before us. Keep your eyes on Jesus, our leader and instructor. He was willing to die a shameful death on the cross because of the joy he knew would be his afterwards; and now he sits in the place of honor by the throne of God. If you want to keep from becoming fainthearted and weary, think about his patience as sinful men did such terrible things to him. (Heb. 12:1–3 TLB).*

Remember the old watch commercial that said, "Timex—takes a licking and keeps on ticking!" Not a bad description of perseverance!

Motivation, inspiration, and target—the M.I.T. factors—make possible personal endurance. To persevere, we must be able to answer three questions:

1. What is my motivation for pursuing the course I'm on?
2. What sources of inspiration will keep me on course?
3. Where is my target?

How you answer these questions can give you the fuel you need to keep your high-octane efforts moving forward.

A modern fable tells about a dog that loved to chase other animals. He bragged about his great running skill and said he could catch anything. One day a mild-mannered rabbit put his boastful claims to the test. With ease the little creature outran, outturned, and outmaneuvered his barking pursuer. The other animals, watching with glee, began to laugh. The dog excused himself, however, by saying, "You forget, I was running only for fun. He was running for his life!" That does make a difference!

Motivation makes all the difference. Saint Francis of Assisi said, "No one will ever know the full depth of his capacity for patience and humility as long as nothing bothers him. It is only when times are troubled and difficult that he can see how much of either is in him." When nothing seems to help, think of the stonecutter. He hammers away at the rock, perhaps a hundred times, without as much as a crack to show for all his effort. Yet at the hundred and first blow it splits in two—and he knows it was not the final blow that did it, but all the others that had gone before.

George Matheson said, "To lie down in the time of grief, to be quiet under the stroke of adverse fortune, implies a great strength. But I know of something that implies a strength greater still. It is the power to work under stress, to continue under hardship, to have anguish in your spirit and still perform daily tasks. This is a Christ-like thing. The hardest thing is that most of us are called to exercise patience, not in the sick bed, but in the street."

Awards get distributed at the finish line. To be able to persevere, to be able to endure, and move forward—that's winning. It's not where you start or even how you start that matters, but how you cross the finish line. Don't be remembered for what you quit because you are weak, but rather what you endured because you are strong.

We have to exercise self-control, training, and perseverance every day. We press on every single day despite the stress. And here's what happens. Over time, one day, we'll wake up and discover we have abilities we never dreamed we'd have. And it doesn't stop there. The more self-control, the more training, and the more perseverance we employ, the stronger we get.

Never ask God to do for you what you must do for yourself. You find true spirituality when you get in alignment with how God works in your life and press on with courage and determination.

PRESS ON TO THE GOAL

A defining moment in every race comes when we're tempted to stop, slow down, or slump over in defeat. Runners call it "hitting the wall." It comes at a point in the race when they have run too far to turn back, but not far enough to win anything. Everything in the race gets decided in that moment. Will they quit or press on?

Let me suggest three things to help you press on when you hit the wall and think you can't go on. When you feel tempted to stress out, remember to pace yourself, brace yourself, and grace yourself.

Be Sure to Pace Yourself

When I filled out the entry form for the 10K race, I answered several questions untruthfully. I lied about my weight and I lied about how long I had been running. I know these little white lies speak to my vanity, but my third lie revealed my stupidity. I lied about how fast I could run the race.

Although I didn't know it at the time, the answer to this question determined my position on the starting line. It never occurred to me that where I started would determine not only how I finished, but if I finished at all.

As a young and dumb athlete, I knew I wouldn't finish with the fastest runners, but I did at least want to get a picture of me starting with them. So I lied and officials believed me. I moved to the front of the line and there stood shoulder to shoulder with some runners from Africa—and right then and there I knew I'd made a bad choice. These guys looked anorexic next to me—long, lean, angular, and muscular. You would look at them and think, *Built for speed,* and then turn and look at me and think, *Built for comfort.* I looked as if I'd just come out of the New Balance store with all my new duds on. They looked as if they'd just come off the trail.

And our differences didn't stop with the cosmetic.

When the starting gun sounded, they glided off like a group of gazelles. I galloped like a mule, straining to pull a plow. I tried to keep up with these guys and did . . . for about fifty feet. Even running as fast as I could, I couldn't run their pace. I needed to be back with the plodders who ran a pace similar to mine.

When we run with people who run at our pace, we all run faster. We start pressing each other at our pace. If you're trying to run your life at someone else's pace, stop it! You're not ready for that kind of stress. Remember that while overstress kills, right-stress builds.

Since that day I've learned about pacing from my wife, Paula. I live with a woman who can work twenty-three hours a day. I used to try to keep up with her until one day I remembered my 10K running experience, and then I said, forget it! I'm not in competition with my wife. We're partners for life. We're in this race together and it's okay that we don't run at the same pace or even in the same way. I found deliverance from self-imposed guilt the day I admitted that by 9:30 P.M., my physical and emotional batteries had run out, while my wife, God bless her, is just getting her second wind. I can't run at her pace, and God doesn't expect me to. What freedom!

You don't have to run my race, and I don't have to run yours. We don't all start at the same place; so stop judging yourself by the people ahead of you or behind you.

Be Sure to Brace Yourself

Life in the real world can get real hard real quick. John Wesley, the founder of the great Methodist movement, said, "Men, never despair, but if you do, work on in despair." And Jesus himself warned, "I have told you these things, so that in me you may have peace. In this world you will have trouble. But take heart! I have overcome the world" (John 16:33 NIV).

All of us face mountains that seem to come up out of nowhere. Trying to avoid them won't work, and trying to ignore them can be fatal. I learned something about running up hills the day of my 10K race. I stupidly trained only on a flat, artificial track. About three weeks before the big day, I started running ten miles every other day on this track. I'd read that such a routine would prepare me to run the 10K faster. So I ran ten miles on a track—and not until race day did it dawn on me that I would be running on anything but a flat track. I would have to run on city streets, up and down some major hills. The only nice thing about running a hill is that once you get to the top, you can coast down the other side—unless, as in this case, it leads to a bigger hill.

Trust me, when you're training for your race in the real world, train for the hills.

Be Sure to Grace Yourself

After his presidency ended, Ronald Reagan confessed, "You know, by the time you reach my age, you've made plenty of mistakes if you've lived your life properly." Saint Francis of Sales repeated the same sentiment in different words: "Be patient with everyone, but above all with yourself."

You're going to make mistakes, and some will be doozies! You're going to fall and you're going to falter, so grace yourself. I love verse 3 of Psalm 130: "If you, O LORD, kept a record of sins, O Lord, who could stand?" (NIV). The answer? No one!

Take into account not only the dumb things you do to yourself, but also a sobering warning from Scripture: "Be careful—watch out for attacks from Satan, your great enemy. He prowls around like a hungry, roaring lion, looking for some victim to tear apart" (1 Pet. 5:8 TLB). Lighten up on yourself, because you can't know when you might wake up with a bad case of the "stupids." I know, because I broke out with the full-fledged disease during my big race.

The race fell on one of the hottest days of the year. By race time, the temperature had soared to the mid-nineties, accompanied by high humidity. As I ran, I noticed that several fire hydrants gushed cool water onto the roadway. The sight of that cool, clean water pouring into the streets provided a temptation I couldn't resist. I ran through the first one and it felt great. I thought, *Now, this is the ticket. If I can run through enough of these, I'll have it made in the shade.* It brought great, temporary relief from the oppressive heat; I could even see the steam rising off my shoes!

I thought it was all just too cool—until it dawned on me that none of the serious runners seemed to be running through the hydrants. I dismissed it at first. Then I started thinking, *There has to be a reason why only guys who look like me are running through the hydrants.* After passing through about four or five hydrants, I looked down and asked myself, "Did I start out with pink socks? I don't remember putting on pink socks." I also began to feel some pain. Before long, a red bubble started oozing up through my shoelaces. Then it hit me why the experienced runners avoided the fire hydrants. The friction between my feet and my wet socks and shoes began to form blisters on both feet. I had blisters on the tops of my feet, on the bottoms of my feet, even between my toes. It felt as though I were running on two pieces of raw meat and my water-logged socks and shoes made me feel as though I were wearing anvils. And too late I thought, *How stupid can one person be?*

Have you ever awakened with a case of the stupids? We all make mistakes, but when you start wearing out the eraser, it might be a clue that something's wrong. When you do something so dumb that you feel tempted to give up, you need to stop and grace yourself. Why hold yourself to a standard that not even God demands? Don't forget, God is a lot easier to please than you are. He looks upon confession of sin as a sign of strength, not weakness.

TRIUMPHING OVER ELBOWS

Although I felt exhausted from running up hills I had not trained for, and even though I limped from blisters I didn't have sense enough to avoid, I felt bound and determined to finish the race.

I distinctly remember coming around a blind curve and seeing the finish line. The mere sight of it gave me a renewed surge of energy. I picked up my pace (or thought I did) until a couple who looked to be in their eighties passed me on my left. Just then I noticed the sweetest voice I'd heard all day. Paula can say my name like no other person in the world. "Come on, you can do it! I see you, baby! You're lookin' good!" Her words got me fired up even more.

With the finish line in sight and my wife's sweet voice ringing in my ears, I lowered my head and made my final push. And it worked. I started gaining on the elderly couple who had just passed me. I vowed that I would pass and defeat these two geriatrics who dared to shame a guy in his mid-twenties by passing him on the way to the finish line. And as God is my witness, as I attempted to pass the old lady on the left, she elbowed me in the chest. And then her husband came up on the right and attempted to trip me. They actually tried to double up on me! And I said to myself, "God, I will die out here today—but these two octogenarians will not beat me."

So I reached back and called on my secret weapon, my STP. I knew that I had self-control, training, and perseverance on my side, so I dug down and found new spring in my step. I forgot about the hills, the blisters, and the lonely hours of training. All I could visualize was crossing that finish line. When I did, it created a lasting memory. I learned something that day I've used in many situations on many other days.

All of us face stress; that is a part of life in the real world. Stress kills some people and strengthens others. You alone can accept the responsibility to choose your attitude, change your aptitude, and control your actions. You alone can pace, brace, and grace yourself. By the grace of God and with a little STP, you can turn stress into strength. Believe me, it's worth going through a little hell in order to feel you've touched a little piece of heaven. And don't let a little elbow stop you.

10

Turning Risk into Reward

You can't escape the responsibility of tomorrow by evading it today.

—ABRAHAM LINCOLN

A big-time movie producer decided to throw a wrap party at his palatial Hollywood mansion to celebrate the completion of what he considered his finest film. Several hundred cast and crew members crowded around his large pool. In order to make the evening more memorable, the producer placed a large white shark—used in shooting the film—into the pool. As a joke, he offered anyone who would swim across the pool $5 million or 5 percent of the movie's net profits.

No sooner had the words left his mouth than guests heard a splash at the far end of the pool. Someone had actually jumped in and began to frantically swim the length of the shark-infested waters. A stunned crowd watched as an audacious young man with a torn and tattered tux pulled himself out of the pool. He looked pale as a ghost and shocked to be alive. The host said, "Well, I never thought anyone would take me up on it—but you did it, and I'm a man of my word. Which do you want, the $5 million or 5 percent of the profits?"

"Right now," replied the reluctant young hero, "I don't care about the money. All I want is the name of the person who pushed me in!"

It's easy to feel pushed into shark-infested waters, because this world is a risky place. You take a risk just by getting out of bed every morning. All of us, at one time or another, have felt as though someone has pushed us into shark-infested waters. At times you may feel as if you work and live around human sharks. Life can be as unforgiving as trying to bungee jump with a log chain.

In an interview with Laurence Fishburne, James Lipton asked, "What does it mean to be an actor and black?"

"Acting is all about risk," Fishburne replied. "You can't act or be an artist, without being willing to live in risk, all the time. On the other hand, being black in America is about being 'at risk.'"

Fishburne made an astute observation on the distinction between living "in risk" and being "at risk." All of us live in risk; that's a part of living in this world. But there's a huge difference between being "in" risk and being "at" risk. At risk means that I live in a dangerous world, on my own and in the minority. And while that can be true, it doesn't have to be. We do not need to be at risk as we live in risk.

God enables us to manage risk; it's his gift to us. He has not left us without means to turn our risks into rewards. Risk-taking introduces the possibility of failing, but it excludes the possibility of becoming a failure. There is a huge difference between the two.

I have a poster of the superstar athlete Michael Jordan hanging on a wall at home. The poster reads, "I have missed more than 9,000 shots in my career. I lost almost 300 games. On 26 occasions I have been entrusted to take the game-winning shot and missed. And I have failed over and over again in my life. And that is why I succeed."

LIVING AT RISK

There is no success without risking failure. Maybe that's why God created us with a neck, because he wants us to stick it out from time to time. The wisest man who ever lived warned us against waiting for risk-free, perfect conditions: "Whoever observes the wind will not sow; and whoever regards the clouds will not reap" (Eccl. 11:4 NRSV).

Thank God for risk-takers such as the Pilgrims and the Founding Fathers of America, or bold presidents who led during times of crisis, such as Abraham Lincoln and Theodore Roosevelt. Thank God for the daring space pioneers such as John Glenn, the sports trailblazers such as Jesse Owens and Wilma Rudolph, and the social reformers such as Rosa Parks and Martin Luther King Jr. If you plan to do anything meaningful with your life, you must get to know the difference between risks worth taking, and those that are not. The former allow you to live confidently while living in risk, while the latter lead you to becoming "at risk."

Let me suggest four risks never worth taking. They represent the four primary risks of the "at-risk" lifestyle.

The Lawless Person Is at Risk

Jan Davis, a sixty-year-old professional parachutist, participated in a dangerous sport called BASE-jumping in which participants illegally parachute off fixed objects like cliffs and towers.

While BASE-jumping on October 22, 1999, Davis fell to her death. Her husband filmed the fatal plunge. Jan was the fourth of five jumpers that day and free-fell for twenty seconds before crashing into the rocks below. Shortly after she jumped off the 3,200-foot granite cliff, El Capitan, in Yosemite National Park, California, her chute failed to open properly.

She and her fellow jumpers knew that they could not legally BASE-jump in Yosemite Park. Legislators adopted the law after BASE-jumping in the park led to six deaths and numerous injuries. Jan and the other four jumpers had come to protest the park's jumping restrictions; ironically, they wanted to prove the safety of their sport. These jumpers not only knew the risks, they also knew the law and deliberately broke it. Jan Davis paid with her life. She lived in risk by virtue of being alive, but she died because of her "at-risk" lifestyle. When she ignored the very laws meant to protect her, she chose to take a risk that cost her everything and gave her nothing.

In a similar way, many people think they can safely violate God's law. But eventually they learn—sometimes the hard way—that God's laws exist for our well-being. We don't break the laws of God; we are broken upon them.

The Loveless Person Is at Risk

To love anything is to risk something. To love someone greatly is to risk that your love might not be returned.

Suppose that after looking, praying, and waiting, you finally find your knight in shining armor. You plan a grand and glorious wedding and a long and loving marriage—but after a few years, he turns out to be an ogre. Or even worse, what if your marriage works, but your spouse dies? I've talked with couples who prayed and planned for years to have a child of their own. God finally blesses them with what they believe to be the perfect child. They love the little one more than life itself. But one day, out of the blue, the child becomes ill and dies of a rare disease. I've tried to comfort brokenhearted parents mourning the death of a young son crushed under the wheel of a hay wagon after he fell off while having fun at a church hayride. I've tried to console a grief-stricken mom and dad after having received news that their daughters died in a freak accident on the way home from a spring-break vacation.

Any one of these scenarios could scare us away from the risks of love. I have sat across from brokenhearted men and women who cry out in pain for a remedy to the brokenness and betrayal of love and friendship. I've heard, and often declared myself, "I'm not going to love anyone ever again. I'm not going to let anyone get that close to me. It's too painful to risk getting hurt that deeply again. I'm just not going to do it anymore."

One definition of parenthood says, "Being a parent is being willing to live, for eighteen years, with your heart on the outside of your body." I'm not sure eighteen is enough. How about a lifetime?

To love anything is to risk pain. But Shakespeare was right when he said, "It is better to have loved and lost, than never to have loved at all." Listen to the value that God puts on love: "There are three things that remain—faith, hope, and love—and the greatest of these is love" (1 Cor. 13:13–14:1 TLB). Only love, of the three Christian virtues, will make it into heaven. There will be no need for faith in heaven and no need of hope. In heaven, love will reign supreme. So to avoid the risk of love and the pain associated with it is to risk never being loved. Now, that's really living "at risk."

The Lyric-Less Person Is at Risk

I have the privilege of living in Music City, USA. The nickname first came from Nashville's status as the home of country music, but the city also has become home to the fastest-growing segment in the music world, Christian music. The truth is, just about every form of music can be found written, performed, and recorded somewhere in Nashville.

The music industry has attracted an abundance of songwriters. To them, nothing sounds better than a well-crafted song that says big things in small spaces. Great lyricists live by the wisdom of Mark Twain, who once said, "The difference between the right word and the almost right word is the difference between lightning and the lightning bug."

Did you know that you're writing lyrics with your life? What story are you telling? If we were to turn your life into a song, would it be, "Your Cheatin' Heart," or "Bad to the Bone," or how about, "I Still Haven't Found What I'm Looking For"? You cannot afford a life without great lyrics.

All great songs have great lyrics. The lyrics usually tell a story, relate an incident, or describe a feeling that touches the heart. These songs have the power to renew our hope, recharge our energy, and refocus our efforts. Like a great song, your life needs to tell a story of who you are, what you believe, what you want to achieve, and how you want to be remembered. It may feel risky to hold strong beliefs and convictions, but the absence of such beliefs will leave the pages of your story empty at best and tragic at worst.

God placed you here, at this moment, to contribute a line, a lyric, a song to the human drama. Which will it be: a charge, an anthem, a battle cry? Or a dirge or a cautionary tale? The poet James Russell Lowell put it this way:

Life is a leaf of paper white
Whereon each one of us may write
His word or two, and then comes night.
Greatly begin! Though thou have time

But for a line, be that sublime—
Not failure, but low aim is crime.

The Legacy-Less Person Is at Risk

Amelia Earhart once said, "Some of us have great runways already built for us. If you have one, take off! But if you don't have one, realize that it's your responsibility to grab a shovel and build one for yourself and for those who will follow after you."

A life without mission is a life without meaning. Meaning gives life direction. A sense of direction creates the hope of arrival at a preferred destination. To see that destination before it appears on the horizon and to want it more than anything is what life is for. Life at its best is about adventure, and to live it fully is to be on a mission that matters.

But like all other things that make life worth living, pursuing a definite mission involves risk. God wants us to go out on a limb sometimes; that's where we find the fruit.

I love the words Luke used to describe the life of King David: "For when David had served God's purpose in his own generation, he fell asleep" (Acts 13:36 NIV). Here we see a classic example of the timeless and the timely. I want to serve that which is timeless and timely. Therefore I love this risk-taker's prayer:

Father, I know that risks must be taken, because the greatest hazard in life is to risk nothing. I know that if I risk nothing, I will lose everything. And if I give nothing, I will receive only leftovers. If I love nothing, I will never know what it's like to be loved. If I avoid the depth of suffering, I'll never know the height of healing. If I refuse to make mistakes, I will never know the exhilaration of learning. If I don't risk changing, I'll be a slave to my past. If I don't risk confessing, I will never know the feeling of being forgiven.

To try boldly is to risk failure, but try boldly anyway. To believe deeply is to risk being wrong; believe deeply anyway. To give generously is to risk your gift being lost; give generously anyway. To sacrifice much is to risk your sacrifice going unnoticed; sacrifice much anyway. To love passionately is to risk not being loved in return; love passionately anyway. Living large may mean you die big; live large anyway. To laugh out loud is to risk appearing the fool; laugh out loud anyway. To weep when wounded is to risk appearing weak; weep anyway. To reach out to another is to risk rejection; reach out to them anyway. To place my dreams, my hopes, and my ideas in front of a crowd is to risk ridicule— but I'm going to dream anyway.

New York theater critic Brooks Atkinson well noted, "This nation was built by men who took risks—pioneers who were not afraid of the wilderness, businessmen who were not afraid of failure, scientists who were not afraid of the truth, thinkers who were not afraid of progress, dreamers who were not afraid of action." Charles Kettering rightly stated, "No one would ever have crossed the ocean if he could have gotten off the ship in the storm." But crossing uncharted waters in order to discover new lands and possibilities makes life wonderful and awe-inspiring. We live in a land discovered and tamed by Pilgrims, pioneers, and faith-filled explorers.

THE REWARDS OF RISK

If those who want to live life fully and dare greatly refuse to live "at risk," then what risks can they rightly take? It seems to me that the risks worth taking are the ones that promise the greatest rewards.

In business we call it ROI, "return on investment." The higher the ROI, the easier it becomes to determine whether the risk has the right reward. We determine the ROI of any risk by asking, "Does God promise to bless this risk?" Consider four risks with a high and eternal ROI.

God Rewards a Wise Risk

A wise risk is the one you don't have to take now, but won't be able to take later. It has a lot to do with timing.

Wise risk-takers understand timing. Wisdom arms me with the knowledge that life is short at best, so I must make the most of every moment. Wisdom also arms me with the power to prevail when I feel "at risk," because I know that God's providence guards my life and "this too shall pass."

The King James Version uses the phrase "It came to pass" 452 times. And while it is merely an archaic way of translating the phrase "It happened," it is still a wise warning. Everything you have goes back in the box. Everything you handle, you're going to hand over. *Someday* is the fool's word for failing to take a wise risk. Jim Elliot, a young missionary martyred for his faith, wisely encouraged others when he said, "He is no fool who gives up what he cannot keep to gain what he cannot lose." Today is the only guarantee you have; wring all the living you can from it.

To risk wisely means to place your life's assets at God's disposal. Find out what God is doing in the world and get in on it. Jesus once told a story about a master who entrusted three servants with three sets of responsibilities. He gave one five thousand dollars, one two thousand dollars, and the last, one thousand dollars. The five-thousand-dollar servant invested the money and brought back ten thousand dollars. The two-thousand-dollar servant invested his resources and brought back four thousand dollars. But the one-thousand-dollar servant dug a hole, put the money in it, and covered it up. He excused his behavior by saying, "I buried it because I know that you are an exacting taskmaster, and I knew that if I lost it, I'd be in deep weeds" (my paraphrase). Jesus said that the master took everything from the last faithless servant and cast him into the outer darkness.

Why get so upset over money? Actually, the money made no difference. The faithless servant feared his fears more than he loved and trusted his master. He confessed that he knew that his master would call him to account.

Smart people understand that while the blessings of God are free, they are not cheap, and certainly do not come without obligation. Losing the financial ROI was not the real risk. Refusing to obey the master placed the servant "at risk."

God Rewards a Willing Risk

God will hold us accountable for whether we use wisely what he has entrusted to us, but he will not force us to act wisely. He simply says, "When your account comes due, I'm not as concerned about what your head and hands have produced as with what your heart is willing to believe."

Wisdom requires that we know what to do, when to do it, and that we do it willingly for the right reason. God doesn't force us to do anything. I've heard people say, "This is my life. I'll do what I want to with it." Fine—but how sad to be that deluded and alone.

Would you like a wake-up call? This is *not* your life; God gave it to you, and life will eventually take it away. Job said, "The LORD gave and the LORD has taken away" (Job 1:21 NIV). The Lord gives, life takes, and God receives. And anything we let go, God gives back, and more. But to believe such a thing requires faith—not faith in faith, but faith in God. It's the principle of investment.

God says to us, "You have to be willing to do this, but I'm not going to force you into it. I'm not going to make you. I'm not looking for robots; I'm looking for friends." Jesus said, "You no longer call me master. I call you friends, because a servant doesn't know his master's heart" (see John 15:15). Jesus says, "You know my heart."

Farmers have to be both wise and willing risk-takers. They know that life operates by the law of the farm, not the law of the factory. The law of the farm says, "Whoever sows sparingly will also reap sparingly, and whoever sows generously will also reap generously. Each man should give what he has decided in his heart to give, not reluctantly or under compulsion, for God loves a cheerful giver" (2 Cor. 9:6–7 NIV).

A woman dying of cancer knew she had little time, but wanted to attend the church picnic. Everyone felt awkward at the presence of this very sick woman, but one by one, they came by to try to console her. One of her friends asked, "Have you thought about your funeral, and how you want it conducted?"

"Yes," she said, "I've told my family I want to be buried with a fork in my hand." A *fork*? the friend wondered. Why a fork?

"When I was a little girl," she said, "I grew up going to church dinners and picnics like this one. Once a year we'd have a homecoming service. There were always lots of good food and glorious desserts. I remember one of the older ladies would say, when they'd come to get our plates, 'Keep your fork, 'cause we've saved the best for last.' It always meant that dessert was coming.

"I want people to know, when they pass by at my funeral and see that fork in my hand, that I understand something good is coming, because God always saves the best for last."

People who willingly take wise risks understand that whatever they let go, whatever they give, God will take and bless and multiply, and then hand right back as something even better.

God Rewards a Redemptive Risk

Do you want to know what God is up to in the world? Then just read this: "For God so loved the world that he gave his only Son, so that everyone who believes in him may not perish but may have eternal life" (John 3:16 NRSV). And he hasn't stopped giving from that moment.

God poured all his resources into one epic act of redemption. The apostle Paul says, "For I owe a great debt to you and to everyone else, both to civilized people and uncivilized alike; yes, to the educated and uneducated alike. So, to the fullest extent of my ability, I am ready to come also to you in Rome to preach God's Good News" (Rom. 1:14–16 TLB). Anything you risk to be a good-news person, God will fund and bless. Helping people get to God is always the right risk.

A redemptive risk means that we never give up on people or on God's desire to see people healed or made whole. This idea came home to me on a Friday morning not long ago when I received a phone call that a young boy from our church had been rushed to the hospital. As I maneuvered my way downtown to the hospital, I thought a lot about how healthy Trevor had looked the Sunday before, sitting down front beside his dad. He looked like the picture of health. When Trevor awakened the next Thursday morning, complaining of common symptoms for his age, his mom wisely allowed him to stay home from school. But by the next morning he wasn't feeling any better.

Thank God, Trevor's mother paid attention to his symptoms and took him to the pediatrician. The doctor, also at the top of his game that day, suspected that Trevor could be showing early signs of a strain of meningitis, so he sent Trevor and his mother to Vanderbilt Hospital. Vanderbilt just happens to be one of the top hospitals in the country dealing with this type of infection. Sure enough, both Trevor's mom and his doctor were right. By the time I arrived around 1:30 that afternoon, Trevor was fighting a strain of meningitis that few, if any, have survived. By the time I made my way back to the pediatric ICU, Trevor looked more like a machine with tubes and hoses than he did a little boy. I felt worthless and helpless, but I knew better than to allow hopelessness to show through, since I've learned that real hope can change things.

With each passing hour, Trevor sank deeper and deeper under the attack of this terrible infection. By this time, the doctors had confirmed that Trevor had contracted meningococcal septicemia. And while I couldn't pronounce it or spell it, I knew that the prognosis seemed bleak. Two high-profile cases of this infection already had made the news in the past several months; both cases had ended in tragedy. Trevor had only small odds of surviving even a few days. As I stood with Trevor's mom and dad, all I could think of was how fast life can change. If you're not prepared, life can overtake and overwhelm you.

For the next several days, I visited Trevor. And with each visit, the hopes that Trevor would recover lessened. Early that next Sunday morning I received word that in a last-ditch effort to save Trevor, the doctors gave him an experimental drug that had been used in only a handful of dire cases. I didn't want to give up on the hope that maybe God would do something, if we took the risk to pray for his healing. At each of the services that morning, I informed the people about the situation and called them to prayer for Trevor's healing and recovery. We prayed together, and I asked everyone to gather in groups to pray for Trevor and to call everyone they knew to ask them to pray for him, too.

Later that afternoon, I received word that, about midmorning, Trevor started responding to the medication. Things finally began taking a small turn to the good. By the next day, when I visited Trevor and his family in the hospital, he was making progress and the doctors felt very hopeful. As Trevor's dad and I sat in the hospital cafeteria, I told him what we had done the day before and he informed me of the approximate time Trevor began to respond. We each knew what the other was thinking. God had answered the prayers of thousands of people who dared to risk believing that God cares about eleven-year-old boys. Trevor's survival amazed us all, but his complete recovery is nothing short of a miracle.

We called for redemptive risk that day, a risk called prayer. Not timid or tepid prayer, but storming-the-gates-of-heaven prayer. To pray in faith for someone is to take redemptive risk. Prayer works, but for prayer to work mightily, someone has to be willing to pray and believe mightily. We prayed our simple prayers of childlike faith that morning and God performed a miracle. Would he still have been God if things continued on their natural course? Of course—but the fact remains that a lot of people took a redemptive risk to pray, and God rewarded.

Trevor has fully recovered. He and his dad are playing a lot of golf these days, and I think that's a miracle, too.

It's worth taking the risk to believe in a big God who loves us and who waits to move on our behalf. God rewards a redemptive risk. A redemptive risk covers much more territory than mere physical healing or relational renewal. It is the driving force that causes people to leave their comfort zones and dare to stand up in the marketplace of ideas and need. Maybe it's a person who dares to believe that black children and white children can and should go to school together. Maybe it's the person who dares to believe that a black man and a white man should be able to live in the same neighborhood. How crazy was the person who dared to risk the first open-heart surgery or suggest that a man could and should walk on the moon? More than one person has felt the sting of ridicule for risking such "silly" notions. Yet it turns out that we now regard some of these people who dared to propose such outlandish possibilities as geniuses, revolutionaries, and heroes. And it happened only because they dared to question others and themselves.

Thank God for those who dare to risk their reputations on activities that right wrongs, promote truth over tradition, beauty for brokenness, and make life better for us all.

What wrongs are you trying to right? What risks are you taking for redemption's sake, for you and for those around you? What in your profession, business, family, or church could you help to make better? What risk are you taking to make your relationships healthier?

Only you can decide whether it seems wise to undertake something so ambitious and costly. There will be false starts. You will make embarrassing mistakes along the way. But if you are fortunate enough to have a dream in your heart, be willing to make mistakes in pursuit of it. Dare to be stupid. You just might change the world.

God Rewards Identification Risk

God rewards anyone who risks identifying with him. Jesus put it this way: "And whoever gives even a cup of cold water to one of these little ones in the name of a disciple—truly I tell you, none of these will lose their reward" (Matt. 10:42 NRSV). God says, "Anytime you do anything to identify with me, I am there." Every class you've ever taught matters to God. Every dollar you've ever given to a redemptive cause matters to God. Every prayer you've ever prayed for the broken, bruised, and bored matters to God.

As a youngster, I thought that church was for identifying with God—but the last thing I wanted was to be identified as "religious." I had seen nothing in my childhood that made me want to spend my weekends in church, along with others who didn't seem to want to be there any more than I did.

But I did want to know if anyone up there knew me or loved me. I longed for someone to answer the hard questions that neither I nor the religious people around me could answer. I wanted to know "Why am I here?" and "Why do good people suffer?" and "Why do so many bad things happen to good people?" I had heard that I had a sin problem (the three biggies were smoking, cussing, and cutting class) and that God had a sin-management program for me. Looking back, maybe that's why I would end up leaving church feeling much worse than when I came. It felt like a weekly whipping from God.

My life changed my freshman year in college when God came into my life. Looking back on it now, my conversion seems more like a wooing than a warning. I couldn't be driven to God—listening to screaming preachers proved that—but I couldn't resist being drawn to Christ. When I discovered the grace of God, my life changed forever. When I learned that God willingly came to this earth to identify with me, I took notice. When I heard that God didn't want to make me better, but different, I listened. And today I am so glad I did! Taking the risk to identify with Jesus Christ was the wisest thing I've ever done.

Choosing to identify Jesus Christ as my God and Savior has brought me peace, forgiveness, purpose, joy, and a life filled with meaning and mission. It has not shielded me from the real realities of living in a risky world, but I have never been "at risk" one moment since the day I bowed my head and confessed my need for a Savior.

When I took the risk to identify with Jesus Christ, I embarked on a faith walk that would make my life not just work, but sing. Jesus isn't a distant deity, but an intimate friend. He is my Savior, my healer, my redeemer, and my advocate. He loves me, believes in me, and has a plan for my life that unfolds one day at a time. He has given me the power to prevail, because he has promised that he will never leave me or forsake me. No one—and I mean no one—can come close to all that. I love him, and I trust him with every detail of my life.

So are there no risks to identifying with Christ? I can't say that. I still don't understand a lot of things. Why did God perform a miracle and heal Trevor, but not perform a miracle to heal my dad or my brother? Why does it seem sometimes that God is silent at best and absent at worst? Why do I still struggle with feelings of self-doubt and self-loathing, when I know that God loves me and has forgiven me, both unconditionally and permanently? Why do I still have trouble trusting him even after he has done so much for me and we have such a long history together? I have more questions than answers, but I know this for sure: God can be trusted. That's why I choose to take the right risks. I know that God richly rewards anyone who does so, because he has rewarded me.

THE THRILL OF A FRUITFUL LIFE

Turning risk into reward is God's specialty. You will live in a risky world for the rest of your life, but you do not have to live another day at risk.

Be done with lawless, loveless, lyric-less, and legacy-less risk-taking. Take only the risks that God promises to reward. If you dare to trust God more than you fear what might be ahead of you, you will know the thrill of a highly fruitful life and display the power to prevail.

11

Turning Pain into Gain

God whispers to us in our pleasures, speaks in our conscience, but shouts in our pains: it is his megaphone to rouse a deaf world.

—C. S. LEWIS

In the next few pages I want to explore the idea that pain is necessary. I believe in God, and I accept pain as a part of believing in a good God. It may be hard to explain, but pain is as much a part of life as pleasure. Life yields misery as well as magic. Healing comes after the hurting. And in this world, one could not exist without the other. Pain is a part of the DNA of life in a fallen world.

Here's the reality: if you can't live in a world of pain *with* God, you will live in a world of pain *without* God. You don't get a choice between having pain and being pain-free. You must choose between pain with a purpose and senseless pain. So this is what I believe: God is the teacher, and pain is oftentimes the curriculum.

In the book of James, the half brother of Jesus writes:

Consider it pure joy, my brothers, whenever you face trials of many kinds, because you know that the testing of your faith develops

*perseverance. Perseverance must finish its work so that you may be
mature and complete, not lacking anything. If any of you lacks
wisdom, he should ask God, who gives generously to all without
finding fault, and it will be given to him.* (1:2–5 NIV).

A little later James continues: "Blessed is the man who perseveres
under trial, because when he has stood the test, he will receive the
crown of life that God has promised to those who love him" (1:12 NIV).
We might paraphrase his message, "We should consider it a sheer gift
when tests and challenges come at us, because pressure forces our faith
to the forefront, revealing its true colors."

Some of us shy away from pain because pain means change, and we
hate to change. We welcome things getting better, but we would rather
things stay as they are if they have to get harder before they get better.
We hear that going through pain and surviving it makes us stronger—
but that's one truth we'd rather take by faith than learn from personal
experience.

Yet despite our wishes, pain happens, and when it does, it forever
changes our lives. How we choose to respond to pain holds the key to
becoming the person we want to be, and, more important, closer to the
person God designed us to be.

A Slow Process

Pain changes things, but it does so s-l-o-w-l-y. On the other hand, we
live in a world accustomed to instant change. Slow change is not only
unpopular here, it is downright dreaded.

We want change to be a simple step-through-the-door, push-a-few-
buttons, and presto-change-o, I've arrived—painless, stainless, strainless,
and brainless. That's our preferred path on the road to the good life.

Only one problem: our lives don't work that way. Changing a light-
bulb takes a few minutes, but changing a human heart takes a lifetime.

Two Motivations for Change

Change through pain doesn't only leave us different; it leaves us at a
different place. Like James said, God uses pain to help us "become

mature and complete, not lacking anything." I've noticed that people change under one of two basic conditions.

1. *Some people change because they want to change.* When we change because we want to, we actually change *before* we have to. Usually, arriving at this state of mind happens only after we've felt jolted by something that's happened to someone we know.

Perhaps while staring into the harsh reality of the funeral of a friend your own age, you get a wake-up call that says you should do some things differently. These moments compel us to change because we want to avoid dying young.

2. *The majority of us change only when we have to.* Most of us change only when we have no other choice. This kind of change grabs us around the throat and gets our full attention. When your spouse dies and you go home alone for the first time, you know that every aspect of your life is going to be different. When parents have to bury a child, they recognize the death as an unnatural order of events. After they go home from the funeral, the child's birthdays and holidays still roll around and school still starts each year. Every day and each event provides a cruel reminder that things will never be the same.

This is life-altering change with a "ready-or-not, here-I-come" smash-mouth bite to it. When a major loss leads us into pain, we often end up grieving. It even hurts just to say the phrase: smash-mouth bite.

Many people faced with grief make the mistake of talking about "grief recovery," a term that implies they will regain, restore, and reclaim what they've lost or had to give up. But when life breaks out of the box, there is no putting it back. A different reality has come, a strange, new world. Unwittingly and unwillingly we get thrust into a new reality, where to survive we must adapt. And in these moments we cry out in anguish, "Why me? Why me, Lord? Why should I be having so much of this *joy* that James talked about? What have I done?"

But the real question shouldn't be "Why me?" but, "Why *not* me?"

Kurt Warner, the quarterback for the St. Louis Rams who led his team to its first ever Super Bowl victory, wrote a book titled *All Things Possible*. Warner makes no secret of his Christian commitment, and if you've heard his story you realize that here is a guy, not unlike many, who could stand up and say: "Why me?" This professional athlete achieved one of his lifelong dreams, to make the roster of a professional football team, the Green Bay Packers. Yet a short while later he got cut from the team and wound up stocking grocery store shelves to make ends meet. There he met, fell in love with, and married Brenda, a single mother with two children. One of her children, Zachary, was blind and brain-damaged from a fall in a bathtub when he was a baby. Right after they married, Brenda's parents died in a car wreck.

Warner eventually got a call from the St. Louis Rams to fill in as a third-string, temporary quarterback. And through circumstances that some call fate, Warner became a starting quarterback . . . and the rest is history. During this miraculous year, the *Denver Rocky Mountain News* interviewed him about how he felt about all this adversity. Here's how he responded:

> When I think about my life, I think about my son, Zachary. He is everything to me. He is the most special child I've ever met. Every day is a struggle for him. He just keeps going and he keeps getting better. Zachary falls down really hard at least ten times every day and he gets right back up and he laughs every time. So, when I see Zachary going through what he has to go through, it touches my life to the point that if I throw three interceptions on the football field, it's a joke for me to really get upset, when I see what Zachary has to face every day.[1]

Warner measures his trials and tribulations against the daily trials and tribulations of his son, Zachary, and finds no comparison. Those who can't walk or see would consider it a great privilege to be able to throw an interception or fumble a football.

We know in theory that our time on this earth is limited, so sometimes we find ourselves fixated on the end of our lives instead of enjoying being alive *now*. So we cry out, "Why now, God? Just when I've gotten all my ducks in a row, just when life is going really good, why now do I have cancer, does my child die, does my mother die, do these things happen, do I lose my job?"

Maybe the most important question we can ask is not, "Why now?" but, "What for?" Many times God remains silent, not because he likes to be mean, but because he knows we are looking for a fight, not an answer. What we really want is for God to use his power to restore things to the way they were, to make it just like it was. Isn't it funny that we want God's best, so long as it doesn't disturb the status quo?

Do you remember the story of Dave Dravecky, formerly a pitcher for the San Francisco Giants? He became a National League all-star and pitched in two National League Championships and one World Series game. He seemed on a great path early in his career, when cancer was discovered in his pitching arm. His doctors treated the problem and thought they had cured it. He overcame long odds in recovery and returned to his team, winning his first game back. He wrote a book about his return to baseball, titled *Comeback*.

I recall watching his second comeback game on TV back in 1987, when he took the mound in Montreal, wound up and threw—and the bone in his arm shattered. He ended up losing not only his arm, but also his shoulder. To deal with the pain he wrote a second book titled, *When You Can't Come Back*. He includes an interesting story in that book.

One night a "supersaint" confronted him. Most of us have met one of these saints at some low point in our lives. If you have, you'll never forget it. This one suggested that he had no arm and no shoulder because he didn't have enough faith. He assured him that it was always God's will for all his children to be healed, all the time. And this is how he reflected on the encounter:

> She implied at first that I was suffering because I didn't have enough faith, and then she just outright accused me of not having the faith God wanted for me. That God then had struck me down and I had lost my arm. But her accusations made God into some kind of cosmic vending machine, where if you pushed the right button, you'd get the sweet life free from suffering. Later I learned, as I talked with Christians from around the world, that one of the distinct differences between American Christianity and Christianity as practiced in the rest of the world is this: only in America do American Christians pray for the burden of suffering to be lifted from their backs. In the rest of the world, Christians just pray for stronger backs.[2]

Dravecky has learned to think differently about pain. He has taken control of an unwanted event. His God-honoring, faith-filled, hope-filled attitude has opened his mind to see the upside of suffering. As a result, he is growing stronger through the pain as a responder rather than a reactor who, more interested in feeling victimized, blames God for it or wishes it would just go away. And today he heads a ministry called "Dave Dravecky's Outreach of Hope," a wonderful organization that ministers to those suffering from cancer or amputation.

In his insightful *Sources of Strength,* former President Jimmy Carter told what he learned from his father about how to regard adversity. As a farmer, his father knew the critical place of weather, especially rain, in getting the crops ready for harvest. Carter often heard his father pray for rain, but in the same prayer he heard his father ask for the strength to deal with the continued drought. That has the main elements of perseverance that Dravecky identified: "American Christians pray for the burden to be lifted from our backs. In the rest of the world, Christians pray for stronger backs."

Isaac Singer, who in 1978 won the Nobel Prize for Literature, said, "Life is God's novel, let him write it." I believe we can triumph over trouble if we pray not so much to be protected from dangers, but to find the courage to face them. I love this verse from the book of Romans: "We also rejoice in our suffering, because we know that suffering produces perseverance; perseverance, character; and character, hope" (5:3–4 NIV).

SUFFERING HAS ITS PURPOSE

Does God mean for our suffering to have purpose? Yes, but it would be silly to say that suffering automatically produces stronger, sweeter, healthier, more vibrant, or more vital people. In fact, sometimes suffering produces mean, crusty, bitter, shriveled-up, hateful, hurting people. Why the difference? Again, the difference comes in what you do with your power to choose.

It's not the death of a loved one, blindness, pain, cancer, disability, rejection, or abuse that destroys our lives. What destroys us is self-pity, worry, despair, and hopelessness. Pain pushes us to the lowest ebb, but that's when the tide turns. We are continually arriving at critical turning points. Reinhold Niebuhr recognized that truth when he wrote the now-famous prayer, "God give us grace to accept with serenity the things that cannot be changed, courage to change the things which should be changed, and the wisdom to distinguish the one from the other."

Once more, it comes back to choice. Do we choose *for* life or *against* life? I choose to believe that God has a purpose in all pain. I am convinced we suffer no unnecessary pain *if* we know how to respond to it. I can think of at least three ways God uses pain to shape us.

God Uses Pain to Make Us Better, Not Bitter

If you were to ask someone, "What would be your perfect life?" more times than not you'd likely get a quick response along the lines of, "A perfect life would be filled with endless joy, pleasure, and comfort." But when I hear someone ask for a life filled with endless pleasure, I remember one of the early episodes of Rod Serling's *Twilight Zone*.

A mobster gets gunned down and his soul is transported to the gates of heaven—or at least to his version of heaven. Instead of pearly gates, he comes upon the shiny doors of a magnificent casino. He looks down and sees he is wearing a stylish tuxedo. He looks up and fancily dressed doormen call him by name and pull the doors open wide to allow him to enter. Inside he gapes at the most magnificent casino he has ever seen. A cocktail waitress extends a silver tray with crystal goblets of champagne; he takes one as she tells him the drinks are on the house.

He approaches a gaming table with a roulette wheel. He reaches into his pocket and pulls out a roll of hundred-dollar bills. No matter what he bets, he wins. The same thing happens at the dice table; the same thing at poker; the same thing at blackjack. Every hand is a winning hand, the slot machines always pay off, and he can't roll anything but a seven. The other men in the casino praise his skill, women comment on his good looks and style. He enters the restaurant and dines on sumptuous food with his beautiful new friends. Every day it's the same; every day he wins. He has all he wants to drink, all he wants to eat, and gambles until dawn. This goes on week after week and month after month. One day, the mobster finally goes up to the manager of the casino and says, "You know, I know this is heaven and it's great . . . but maybe God made a mistake sending me to heaven because, you know, after a while . . ."

The manager looks at him and replies, "Oh, no, no, no. God didn't make a mistake. Sir, this isn't heaven. This is your own private hell."

We sometimes think heaven should be, "Dear Lord, let me indulge myself in nothing but pleasure. Just give me all the rights and erase all the wrongs. Just let me gratify myself. That would be heaven, where all the streets are one-way and going in my direction."

But would that really be heaven? Not by a long shot.

God himself administers some of our pain. My wife and I have been blessed with three children, three lovely girls. And we've learned over the years a noticeable difference between children who are confident and accomplished and those who are not. The difference always can be traced to a home that features realistic expectations and boundaries. The writer of Hebrews talks of God's discipline of his children:

> And have you quite forgotten the encouraging words God spoke to you, his child? He said, "My son, don't be angry when the Lord punishes you. Don't be discouraged when he has to show you where you are wrong. For when he punishes you, it proves that he loves you. When he whips you, it proves you are really his child." Let God train you, for he is doing what any loving father does for his children. Whoever heard of a son who was never corrected? If God doesn't punish you when you need it, as other fathers punish their sons, then it means that you aren't really God's son at all—that you don't really belong in his family. Since we respect our fathers here on earth, though they punish us, should we not all the more cheerfully submit to God's training so that we can begin really to live? Our earthly fathers trained us for a few brief years, doing the best for us that they knew how, but God's correction is always right and for our best good that we may share his holiness. Being punished isn't enjoyable while it is happening—it hurts! But afterwards we can see the result, a quiet growth in grace and character. (12:5–11 TLB).

Today we speak more of "discipline" than of "punishment"; it's the more politically correct term. In my younger days as a rambunctious kid in Glasgow, Kentucky, I daily "got on" my mother's nerves. It wasn't called discipline then, either, but a "whuppin'." My brother and I earned our fair share of whuppin's.

In Kentucky we never got very far from the tobacco trade, so we all recognized a tobacco barn yardstick, one of the main tools they used to cure the leaves. It wasn't a flat stick like you see at the hardware store, but a piece of timber about three feet long and an inch and a half square. It looked something like a square broomstick, and one hung in our hall closet—but the one we knew so well had nothing to do with tobacco. I learned early the distinctive sound of the hall closet door opening. Whenever I heard that sound, even when my mother wanted only to fetch the vacuum cleaner, I broke into a cold sweat.

My older brother had a theory: "Show no fear." When Mom had had enough, out came the tobacco stick. She grabbed my brother by the arm and gave him one, two, three swats. My brother never said a word. Not a whimper, not a cry, not a peep. But this show of no fear didn't impress Mom; it simply made her think she needed to get more effective. So in quick succession, he got three more whacks.

When my turn came, she grabbed my arm while I grabbed her shoulder to cut down on her leverage. I started squealing bloody murder even before she touched me. I begged for mercy, confessed my sins, and blathered on about how bad I had been, that I didn't mean it, that I was so sorry, that I wouldn't do it again. Still the whacks came. But by hanging on and staying close, I felt not only the heat of her anger but I saw in her eyes the pain of her disappointment in me. And that hurt far worse than the sting of the tobacco stick.

As I look back I realize that this is how God operates. Sometimes God uses pain to try to make us better. Our choice is simple: Will we get better, will we quit this, will we stop this, will we let this go? Love demands some pain.

God Uses Pain to Build Us Up

In 2 Corinthians 12:7–10 Paul writes about his pain as a missionary:

To keep me from becoming conceited because of these surpassingly great revelations, there was given me a thorn in my flesh, a messenger of Satan, to torment me. Three times I pleaded with the Lord to take it away from me. But he said to me, "My grace is sufficient for you, for my power is made perfect in weakness." Therefore I will boast all

*the more gladly about my weaknesses, so that Christ's power may rest
on me. That is why, for Christ's sake, I delight in weaknesses, in
insults, in hardships, in persecutions, in difficulties. For when I am
weak, then I am strong.* (NIV).

Three times Paul begged God to make him well again, and three
times God said, "No, but I am with you." And that is all we really need.

God's power shows up best in weak people. So Paul gladly boasts
about his weakness; he feels glad to be a living demonstration of Christ's
power. It's like John Banbridge said: "If you haven't got problems, you
should get down on your knees and ask, 'Lord, don't you trust me anymore?'" In all your pain, the will of God will never take you where
God's grace can't reach and keep you.

James Brady, White House Communications Director under President Ronald Reagan, got in the way of an assassin's bullet meant for
the president. Although the bullet ripped through Brady's brain, he
miraculously survived. He underwent months of painful rehabilitation.
He slowly regained his speech, his ability to feed himself, to walk—but
the pain never left his body. Brady refused to sit at home and become
a bitter recluse. Instead, he and his wife, Sarah, have become a constant force in the halls of Congress, lobbying lawmakers for handgun
control. Who could dare challenge his authority to speak on this
subject? He uses his pain as a rallying point, not to ask God for a
"happy" life, but for a life fully responsible, useful, honorable, and compassionate. Sitting in his wheelchair at home, he once told an interviewer, "You gotta play the hand that's dealt you. There may be pain
in that hand, but you play it. And I've played it."[3] Who could argue?
Brady is using his pain to make a noticeable difference that proves he
truly lived.

God Uses Pain to Make Us Mad

I think most of us daily live in some kind of low-level anger. And I
think God sometimes uses pain to get us mad. I mean really MAD!

Remember the great theologian, Paulie, in the movie *Rocky III?*
Clubber Lang is again knocking the stuffing out of Rocky Balboa
and Mickey screams, "He's killing him, he's killing him!" Paulie

reaches over, grabs the mike and says, "He's not getting beat! He's getting mad!"

Sometimes we need to get flat-out mad, and move off of just being angry. Because you know what angry is? A.N.G.R.Y.: **A N**egative **G**rasp on **R**eality and **Y**ourself.

I learned the difference between getting angry and getting mad one summer. As a new ninth grader I had the privilege of trying out for varsity football. In the south, we take football seriously. Football almost represents your right of passage from childhood to manhood. So I had arrived. I was on cloud nine.

That summer I attended football camp. The sun felt hot enough to bake bricks, and there I was, roasting under a helmet and thirty pounds of football pads. But I didn't care. It felt like heaven to me. Coach Butch Gilbert (a cross between a bulldog and a chain saw, and whom to this day I hate with the utmost Christian love) came over to me, sized me up, and decided that I ought to line up against Jerry England.

In our town we had bullies and we had hoods; a hood is a bully on steroids. Jerry England was a full-fledged hood. This guy was big, mean, and tough. I had never met him, but I knew his legend. So we lined up and I assumed my stance, right across from him, and I thought, *This is the largest human being I have ever seen.* He scared me to death. I remember them saying, "HUT!" but that's all. I can't say that it hurt, because I don't remember anything.

When I woke up, I went to the back of the line to start again. That's the way football works: you give your best shot (or in my case, take your best shot), and then you rotate to the back of the line so you aren't across from the same guy repeatedly. But not this time; not with Coach Gilbert. On this day, we matched up against the same guy, over and over again. So once more it was me against Jerry England. But this time I knew what was coming. My body and mind quickly adjusted. I ratcheted up my ability to absorb pain. And when they yelled, "HUT!" I felt everything. Jerry hit me like a freight train. I heard my head rattle around in my helmet and my teeth rattle around in my head. This locomotive of a man hit me so hard my feet flew off the ground, followed by the ground rushing up so hard that it knocked the breath out of me.

It went on like this all afternoon. I would get plastered and slammed, only to get up, dust myself off, and get hammered again. I got knocked down so many times that dusting myself off became a luxury I could no longer afford. Just maintaining consciousness and trying to hear the dreaded bark of "HUT!" over the ringing in my ears seemed challenge enough. That day, Coach Gilbert let Jerry England beat me like a drum. I felt humiliated. I felt defeated.

I felt so afraid, so scared, so beaten up that I waited for everyone else to shower and leave before I took my turn. I hurt! I bled! My throat felt crushed. It felt as though I'd broken my nose. *My football career is over,* I thought. *I wanna go back to beating up seventh graders.*

As I walked by Jerry's locker I said out loud, "You big jerk! Wish you were here NOW!" And then I noticed his jersey, hanging on the locker door. For what reason I don't know, but I pulled out that jersey and looked at the collar to see how big this monstrous man really was. I found the size of the jersey—and I could not believe what I read. I had my jersey in the other hand and I put it up next to his, and guess what? We wore the same size.

Something inside me changed at that moment. I got mad! I said, "He ain't that big! If he can fit in this jersey, which I can barely fit into, I'm mad!"

Instantly I felt **M**otivated to **A**ct **D**ecisively—and I made the team. I lettered that year, but Jerry England still beat me senseless in practice every day. But I am a better, stronger, and more resilient person today because I decided to get mad and move off of just being angry. I stopped feeling indignant and did something about it. Ralph Waldo Emerson once said, "Our greatest glory consists not in never falling, but in rising every time we fall." That was the lesson I learned going into ninth grade, and I carry it with me to this day.

Sometimes I think God is trying to get some of us mad! Sometimes God is trying to get us motivated to act decisively, instead of just sitting there and blubbering about our lives.

Again, it all comes down to choice. You either choose to grow through the pain, or you start to die because of it.

GOD'S HANDS, OUR HANDS

I'd like to close this chapter by telling a true story of an ordinary man who suffered an almost simultaneous loss of love and life. He chose to live through the pain, and by so doing, he unknowingly became God's hands.

He was a big bear of a man, with a booming hello and an even louder laugh. Over the years he had built a thriving construction business. Eventually the time came to think about selling his company and moving toward retirement. He had plenty of good offers to consider, and he took his time to choose the company that most closely reflected his own values. The buying company insisted upon a multiyear employment contract with the seller in order to help oversee the transition of clients and to help bring in new business.

Shortly after the sale, the man learned that his only son had died by suicide. His friends and family and business acquaintances immediately came to his side, but they really couldn't understand the pain of a father whose twenty-something son took his own life. A blackness descended upon the man's soul, threatening to blot out his own life. Day after day he prayed to God. He lifted his pain up to the Lord and in anguish cried out, "Why, God? Why my son? Why now?" And there came no answer, no response, no sign. Just silence.

After several weeks of mourning, this man began to pour himself back into his job. Slowly, ever so slowly, the darkness lifted, and he began moving into what he describes as a gray twilight. He lived there for more than a year. The strain proved too much for his marriage, which ended quietly in divorce. Again his plaintive prayers of "Why, God? Why now? Why me? What for?" went unanswered.

Almost two full years to the day after his son's death, he received a phone call from an established client regarding the construction of a huge new distribution facility. Meetings were held, construction plans drawn up, contracts signed, and work started on this multimillion-dollar job. A few weeks into the project, he started noticing schedules slipping, phone calls not being returned, and faxes going unanswered.

So the man made a trip to his client's corporate headquarters to meet with the project architect. But instead of seeing the vibrant, energetic young man he had known, he saw a bedraggled, unkempt, unshaven version of the same man. The young architect apologized profusely for his appearance and for allowing the project to slip behind schedule, then sat down and began to weep. The young man recounted how he and his wife had discovered their only son had cancer. He was spending all his time at the hospital and feared he would have to resign from the company or take extensive family medical leave. As the key architect on the project, he knew such a decision would delay construction of the distribution center for almost a year and almost certainly roadblock his career. "I just don't know what to do," he moaned.

The older man walked across the office, placed his hands in the hands of the architect and said, "You go be with your son, go be with your family, go and be by his hospital bed. Don't worry about the distribution center and don't think about resigning. I'll handle it. Give me this burden."

The older man rolled up the construction plans and went back to his office. He handed off all his projects to other engineers so he could concentrate on the distribution center. He constantly burned up the cell phone to make sure the young architect knew of all the major decisions and changes that had to be made. The architect's son eventually responded to treatment, and his doctors pronounced the boy's cancer in complete remission. During the last month of construction, the architect came back on-site and greeted the president of the company for the distribution center's grand opening—on schedule and within budget.

Of course, the young man felt forever grateful to his new friend, not only for standing in the gap, but also for giving him precious time to be with his son when his son needed him most. In a letter of thanks he wrote, "My wife and I prayed for God to grant us a miracle, and within a week of that prayer, you walked in the door and made all the difference in the world." The man had never before thought of himself as an answer to prayer. A few months later he was the guest of honor at the boy's eighth birthday party.

But that's not the end of the story.

Within a year of completing the distribution center, the man met a senior official to discuss construction of a new hospital for a midsize city. The dinner conversation felt stiff and stilted. Every time the man tried to engage his prospective client in meaningful discussion, the talk became disjointed and trailed off.

Finally, the man gently asked, "What's the problem here?" The hospital official apologized and said slowly, "A few weeks ago . . . my son committed suicide."

The statement hit like a sledgehammer. The dinner suddenly became incidental as the two men discovered a terrible bond. The minutes passed into hours, and by the time they parted company, they promised to keep in touch, not merely about building the hospital, but to help each other through the tough times of holidays, birthdays, and the lonely morning hours when sleep flees.

That evening the man experienced a tremendous healing. He actually felt as though he had become God's hands. To commemorate his healing, the man had two sayings cross-stitched and hung on the walls of his office:

The deepest darkness cannot extinguish the light
of even the tiniest candle.
    and
I have often been adrift, but I have always stayed afloat.

Pain and suffering may from time to time set us adrift, but we need to hang on to our faith in God's love and grace. And that faith will buoy us up in stormy seas. I beg you, in God's name, don't turn away from him, despite whatever pain you may feel. Don't think of your loss as a vicious thing from him. It can be a redemptive thing, meant for your good.

God is so big and so good and he has the power not only to touch every heart, but also to heal every pain. And if we choose life during our times of deep darkness, then we will reach out and find ourselves securely in God's hands. And sometimes, he lets us be his hands for someone else.

12

Turning Failure into Fertilizer

The conditions of conquest are always easy.
We have but to toil awhile, endure awhile, believe always,
and never turn back.

—MARCUS ANNAEUS SENECA

How do people prevail in the face of extraordinary and repeated adversity? Colin Powell, the great American military and political leader, got it right when he offered this response to the question "To what do you attribute your success?"

"There are no secrets to success," he replied. "It is the result of preparation, hard work, and learning from failure."

Yet Americans fear failure. Our success-oriented society frowns on failing and celebrates winning. But as painful and embarrassing as failure is, it can be a great teacher if you know how to use it. In fact, failure has served as your teacher more times than you may like to remember.

Think back to your childhood. You fell down the first time you tried to walk. You sank the first time you tried to swim, and you probably struck out the first time you got up to bat. Even heavy hitters, the ones who hit the most home runs, also strike out the most. Ted Williams, at the height of his professional career, made an out 6 times out of 10. R. H. Macy failed 7 times before his store in New York caught on. English novelist John Creasey got 753 rejection slips before he published 564 books. Babe Ruth struck out 1,330 times, but he also hit 714 home runs.

The apostle Paul gave some good advice when he said, "So don't get tired of doing what is good. Don't get discouraged and give up, for we will reap a harvest of blessing at the appropriate time" (Gal. 6:9 NLT). Some people fear failure so much they become overly cautious to the point of disconnecting from real life. They follow a policy of guarded living and holding back time, talents, and treasure from the service of God or man. Their motto is: To keep from failing—don't try!

Thank God, many others willingly make mistakes and risk failure on the way to doing great things. Instead of shrinking back in fear, they go forward in faith. They see every problem as an opportunity. And while they may fail many times along the way, these courageous people would rather fail temporarily at something bound to succeed, than succeed at something ultimately doomed to failure. Benjamin Franklin once said, "The man who does things makes many mistakes, but he never makes the biggest mistake of all—doing nothing."

THREE INGREDIENTS OF FAILURE

Failure is no mystery. We fail at some things for real, legitimate reasons. I've observed three common reasons for why we fail: circumstance, lack of competency, and absence of character.

Some Failure Is Circumstantial

Suppose you plan a gigantic picnic as the center of this year's family reunion. You organize everything perfectly. You arrange the food by meat, bread, vegetable, dessert, and drink. You take into account all ages for the games you plan. You leave nothing to chance—but because you can't control the weather and it rains, the picnic flops. What can you do?

Or let's say you want to start a business. You practice "due diligence" by researching the market thoroughly. You identify all the players in the market. Armed with the knowledge, you craft a masterful business plan. You launch the business with all the enthusiasm you can muster and the initial response seems encouraging, but without warning, the bottom falls out of the market. Or you find a hot market and high demand for your idea, but you can't find the right people and resources to make it work.

What happened in all these examples? The ventures failed due to circumstances beyond anyone's control. The best-laid plans of mice and men do sometimes go astray.

Failure from without is an unfortunate fact of life. You can't escape it, but if you wait for all the circumstances to line up in your favor, you will wait until it becomes too late. I believe in long-range planning, but I also believe that long-range plans are useless. The quickest way I know to get God to laugh is to tell him your plans. And if you really want to prompt some cosmic comedy relief, show him your timetable. Only God knows the time and the season.

Some Failure Comes from Incompetence

Without the skill to do what you're attempting to do, you will fail. If you don't have a set of competencies that match the task, you won't succeed.

Of course, if you don't have the necessary competencies, most of the time you can gain them. All of us ought to become lifelong learners. We can grow. We can get smarter as we work harder. An old German proverb says, "To change and change for the better are two different things." By choosing your attitude and changing your aptitude, you can gain the knowledge to start again, this time smarter and wiser. It's never too late to gain the knowledge and skills you need to succeed.

Some Failure Comes from Lack of Character

I've seen more failure on the basis of character issues than of all the circumstantial and competency issues put together. Over the years I've watched too many people work hard and sacrifice long to achieve a level of notoriety and success that they have no way of sustaining. How sad to watch a person whose gifts have taken them places their character can't keep them.

Over time, none of us behave in a way different from how we truly see ourselves. If we don't respect ourselves, then whatever level of success we achieve, we will sooner or later self-destruct. On the outside things may look together, but on the inside a little voice says, "I don't deserve it."

We cannot sustain ourselves at a level of success that outstrips our level of character. Everyone wants success, but not everyone prepares for it. The burden of success carries many responsibilities. That's why the key to character is trust.

According to the Bible, we build a trusted character over time, not overnight. It comes through a process, not a position. And it focuses on progress, not perfection. As Phillips Brooks noted, "Character may be manifested in the great moments, but it is made in the small ones."

We find character in the inner man or woman. Pursuing success without first taking the time to build a strong inner life is like trying to build a skyscraper using a shallow foundation. To go higher, you first must go deeper. Any other approach depends on ego rather than character, and ego doesn't have enough stuff to fill a hole that big.

Character also means that we're being wise and willing to gain perspective before we act. One careless act can undo a lifetime of careful decision making. And once we lose or diminish character, we cannot recover it merely by saying a prayer.

Too many people have such an incomplete picture of God's grace that they think they can ignore issues of spiritual maturity, then act with impunity, expecting God to give them a "do-over." The movie *City Slickers* illustrates such a misguided notion. Three guys decide to regain the glory years of their youth by spending two weeks on a dude ranch just before their fortieth birthdays. Billy Crystal plays Mitch, Daniel Stern plays Phil, and Bruno Kirby plays Ed. One night during the cattle drive, Mitch and Ed find a distraught Phil in his tent, playing with a gun. Eventually Phil opens up to Mitch and Ed:

PHIL: I'm at a dead end. I'm almost forty and I've wasted my life.

MITCH: Yeah, but now you have a chance to start over. You remember when we were kids and we'd be playing ball, and the ball would get stuck up in the tree or something? We'd yell, "Do-over!" Your life is a do-over. You've got a clean slate.

PHIL: I've got no place to live. I'm going to get wiped out in the divorce 'cause I committed adultery, so I may never even see my kids again. I'm alone. How does that slate look now?

Failure from within is hard to explain, but the signs are easy to spot.

A FAILURE MIND-SET

Failure is a way of thinking long before it becomes a way of acting. Like most things, failing over time becomes a habit. A habit merely acts out a way of thinking. When people fail over time, they take on a failure mentality. And a failure mind-set generally takes on four deadly characteristics: avoidance, blame-placing, apathy, and playing not to lose.

The Plague of Avoidance

People with a failure mentality avoid things they don't like. They expertly dodge responsibility and run from reality.

We live in a no-fault society. Everyone tries to blame someone else for the mess they're in. It seems like a national pastime to avoid taking personal responsibility. But when you and I refuse to look at ourselves honestly and admit that we are responsible for what we do, we set ourselves up for failure—and not just one, but an entire string of failures that can stretch over many months, years, and even an entire lifetime.

People with a failure mentality avoid taking responsibility by shifting it to others. They delve deeply into denial because they can't or won't confront the glaring and obvious problem that everyone else sees but them—like a pink elephant on the couch that no one wants to acknowledge. We hope that if we avoid the issue, maybe it will go away.

Such a glaring character weakness tends to repeat itself over and over. If you lean toward avoidance, dig up the root or you'll continue to grow the fruit.

The Bane of Blame-Placing

People who fail repeatedly tend to develop a victim's mentality. They love to say, "It's not my fault." Because they have chosen to be a victim, they shift the blame to someone else, usually someone who's absent.

But they ought to spell blame, "Be-lame!" Lame people limp through life looking for someone on whom they can hang the cause of their woes. They convince themselves that they could never be the source of their own failures. It's the fault of their parents, their teachers, or their boss. It's never them. It might be the way their mother held them or the way their brother yelled at them, but never them. They cry, "They won't let me," or "They're keeping me down," or "Those people over there hurt me!"

I saw this mind-set illustrated not long ago in a note on a bulletin board of a break room: "This office requires no physical fitness program. Everyone gets enough exercise jumping to conclusions, flying off the handle, running down the boss, knifing friends in the back, dodging responsibility, and pushing their luck." How sad to play the victim with victory within reach!

The Curse of Apathy

A guy took a survey seeking to answer the question "Some people believe the biggest problems facing America are ignorance and apathy. Would you agree or disagree?" A harried businessman waved off the question with a terse, "I don't know and I don't care."

Despite all our blessings and benefits, we live in a chronically cynical world. We live in a critical culture. You can't turn on the TV without listening to highly paid talking heads tell us how bad things are and who's to blame for it. When I'm tempted to fall into cynicism and apathy, I reread Theodore Roosevelt's advice concerning critics:

It's not the critic who counts, not the man who points out how the strong man stumbles, or where the doer of deeds could have done better. The credit belongs to the man who is actually in the arena, whose face is marred by dust and sweat and blood, who strives valiantly, who errs and comes up short, again and again, because there is no effort without error and shortcoming. Who does actually try to do the deed, who knows the great enthusiasm, the great devotion and spends himself (or herself) in a worthy cause? Far better it is to dare mighty things to win glorious triumphs, even though checkered by failure, than to rank with those poor spirits who neither enjoy nor suffer much because they live in the gray twilight that knows neither victory nor defeat.

You can't afford the indulgence of feeling sorry for yourself And anyway, it doesn't do an effective job of gaining you any sympathy.

The pit of self-pity is a lonely place. Few individuals will willingly descend into that pit with you. Even Winston Churchill felt the sting of the critic's pen and the fickle nature of popularity. Once, after he gave a speech that attracted an audience of ten thousand, a friend asked, "Winston, aren't you impressed that ten thousand people came to hear you speak?" Churchill replied, "Not really. One hundred thousand would come to see me hang."

The Scourge of Playing Not to Lose

Carl Wallenda, one of the greatest tightrope aerialists who ever lived, once wrote, "For me, to live is being on a tightrope. All the rest is waiting." In 1968, he declared that the most important thing about walking a tightrope is to be confident you can do it and never to think about failure. Yet in 1978, Wallenda fell to his death from a tightrope seventy-five feet above the city of San Juan, Puerto Rico.

His wife, also an aerialist, reported that for three months prior to attempting the most dangerous feat he'd ever tried, Carl spoke only about falling. Never before in all their career together, she said, had Carl ever given a thought to falling. She noted that he spent all his time prior to that fatal walk putting up the wire (something he had never bothered with). He worried about the guide wires and spent endless hours calculating the wind, another thing he had never done. After his death, she said, "I believe the reason Carl fell was because he spent all of his time preparing not to fall, instead of spending time preparing to walk the rope."

In life you tend to create what you focus on. If you constantly think about failure, then how can you produce anything but failure?

We fail when we don't live up to our God-given potential. We fail when we lack the self-discipline to give a venture our best shot. There is a lot to be said for trying. If we are doing the best we can with the skills and knowledge we possess, and if we make the best use of the resources available to us, then we win.

That doesn't mean, of course, that we will always take the blue ribbon. Whoever crosses the finish line first, we name the winner. But where does that leave all those who come in second, third, or thirteenth? As losers or failures? No! I refuse to believe that only those who win gold medals or who wear Super Bowl rings are winners.

You have heard the old saying "If at first you don't succeed, try, try again." Maybe it ought to read, "If at first you don't succeed, don't be surprised."

GOD CAN USE FAILURE

We may not like failure, but God likes to use it to make us into successes beyond our wildest dreams. Consider the story of how Jesus challenged Peter and his brother Andrew to a new venture.

These veteran fishermen had been fishing all night without success. No doubt they felt like utter failures early that morning. Instead of selling fish and counting money, they filled their time with cleaning nets and making excuses. Jesus took note of their failure but asked them to launch back out in the deep for a catch. At this point they had to make a pivotal choice: to change and learn, or avoid the issue, place the blame on the nets, and descend into apathy.

God Uses Failure to Stop Our Progress

Sometimes God lets us fail because we're heading down the wrong road or doing the wrong thing. How many times have I begged God for something I thought I must have, and then blamed him for ignoring me when I didn't get it? But thank God, he loves me enough to let me fail in order to stop my progress down the wrong road.

God doesn't throw us away when we crash through carelessness or outright defiance. The pain caused by adultery, lying, cheating, or whatever, still hurts. You can't flippantly walk through life thinking, *Well, I'll go do this, and then God will forgive me.* Yes, he will forgive you, but think of all the collateral damage you'll cause. Stop and count the cost! I like to pray, "Dear Father, if I'm going down the wrong road, stop me. And please, Lord, stop me early and not too late."

Life with God is not a "do-over." You can, by God's grace, begin again—but let's face it, life is too short to go back and start over too many times. To wean us from the "do-over" mentality, God disciplines us: "The Lord disciplines those he loves" (Heb. 12:6 NIV). If God isn't disciplining you—if God isn't saying "no" and stopping your progress in the wrong direction—please beg him to begin.

Paul commended one group of young believers by rejoicing that they had "turned to God from idols to serve the living and true God" (1 Thess. 1:9 NIV). What a vivid example of the biblical idea of repentance! To repent means to change your mind about the direction you're going and to turn around and go in the other direction. God uses failure to get us to do a 180.

God refuses to say "yes" when love demands a "no." When a child you love is going down a road that you know leads to great pain and heartache, love demands discipline. Not punitive discipline, but the kind that calls for the loved one to stop and do a 180. Every parent knows this. Any parent who says, "Oh, I just love my children too much to discipline them," is fooling themselves. Jesus observed that even human fathers know love sometimes demands that they say "no" to the very things they know will end up hurting the people they love (Matt. 7:9).

Failure doesn't mean you have been a fool. It proves you had faith enough to try. Failure doesn't mean you are inferior. It just means you're human, like the rest of us. Neither does it mean that you've wasted your life or that you should give up or that you'll never make it. And it certainly does not mean that God has abandoned you. It may simply mean that God loved you enough to keep you from hurtful success in the short run so that you can genuinely triumph in long run.

God Uses Failure to Starve Our Pride

Jesus certainly knew that his counsel to Peter and Andrew about fishing had to hurt their pride. After all, they were the professionals, not him. But sometimes human pride needs a hole or two poked in it.

Jesus looked at Peter and said, "Go back out, and cast your nets on the side opposite of where you normally fish." Peter replied, "Master, we've worked hard all night and haven't caught anything" (Luke 5:5 NIV). Still, after stating the obvious, Peter submitted. By doing so he came under the blessing of grace: "But he gives us more grace. That is why Scripture says: 'God opposes the proud but gives grace to the humble'" (James 4:6 NIV).

Pride puffs up before it brings low. Peter could have said, "We've never done it that way before," or "We tried that and it didn't work," or "No respectable fisherman would cast a net on that side of the boat," or (this one would have been a real hoot) "Who made you God?" But, thank God, Peter willingly stopped his way and started again God's way.

Alexander Graham Bell said, "Sometimes we stare so long at a door that is closing that we see too late the one that is open." Peter and the disciples willingly swallowed their personal injury over the "closed door" of fishless nets to accept the "open door" right in their midst—Jesus the Christ.

God Uses Failure to Transfer Our Trust

Peter was smart enough to say, "Okay. We have fished all night with nothing, but . . . at your word . . ." (Luke 5:5). Peter faced a choice. Who would he trust? He placed his confidence in Christ and reaped results beyond his wildest imaginings.

Success comes from obedience to the words of Jesus. John Calvin in his commentary on this verse says that "Christ showed his power, first, in their taking so large a draught of fishes, and secondly, when by his hidden power he preserved the net which must otherwise have been torn and burst."

Jesus wanted to teach Peter to trust him. And it didn't take long for his trust to be validated by spectacular results.

Sometimes, God lets us fail in order to remind us, "Whom do you trust? Are you trusting your job? Are you trusting your skills? Or are you trusting me?" I have clung to the promise of the following verse like a drowning man clings to a life preserver: "As the Scripture says, 'Anyone who trusts in him will never be put to shame'" (Rom. 10:11 NIV). Stop trying to figure everything out and trust that God already has it all figured out. Then you, too, will be able to bear witness to the truth of another great verse: "You will keep in perfect peace him whose mind is steadfast, because he trusts in you" (Isa. 26:3 NIV).

On the day of this miracle, the disciples laid their boats, their nets, and their fish down, and didn't return until after Christ's crucifixion, and then only for a short time. Isn't it interesting that what Peter and the other disciples used to think so important and central faded into the background when Christ came on the scene? In one instant his blessing changed their priorities.

If the blessings of God have not made you more in love with Christ and more willing to trust him, then you have missed the point. Why would anyone waste their time crying over empty (or even full) fishing nets, when the one who created the fish and who knows all their tendencies and swimming patterns is standing in their presence, offering his help? Who wants to play with a superman doll when the living God-man is in the boat?

God Uses Failure to Grow Us Up

I vividly remember when my children had to learn how to tie their shoes. Whenever I attempted to help them they invariably said, "I can do it; I can do it myself. Leave me alone. Quit it! Stop it!" So I let them wear themselves out. Pretty soon, I'd hear a shy, timid voice saying, "Daddy, would you please tie my shoe?"

Tom Watson Sr., the founder of IBM, had a junior executive who spent $12 million on a project that didn't work. The young man placed his resignation on the founder's desk, sure that Watson would be expecting it. Watson replied, "You can't quit. I've spent $12 million training you. Now get to work."

Henry Ford said, "Failure is the opportunity to begin again more intelligently." Failing doesn't mean you are a failure, just that you haven't yet succeeded. Failing doesn't mean you have accomplished nothing. It means you've learned what not to do. Thomas Edison once searched for a workable filament for his incandescent lamp. In his search he conducted ten thousand experiments without finding a solution. A reporter asked him how he could continue to forge ahead despite so many failures. "If I find ten thousand ways something won't work," Edison replied, "I haven't failed. I am not discouraged, because every wrong attempt discarded is another step forward. Just because something doesn't do what you planned it to do doesn't mean it's use-less." Thomas Edison had grown up. He knew that only one thing counted as failure, and that was quitting.

DESTINED TO WIN

Failure-prone folks often say, "If at first you don't succeed, destroy all the evidence that you ever tried." But a wiser man once defined real fail-ure like this: "living without knowing what life is all about, feeding on things that do not satisfy, thinking you have everything, only to find out in the end you have nothing that matters."

Take away my capacity for pain, and you rob me of the possibility for joy. Take away my ability to fail, and I would not know the meaning of success. Let me be immune to rejection and heartbreak, and I could not know the glory of living.

I challenge you to get up off your good intentions, get in the battle, and stay with it. Take the best you are, along with the best you have, and do the best you can. As long as you keep trying, even though others tell you it's hopeless, you will never be a loser. Abraham Lincoln said, "My great concern is not whether you have failed, but whether you are con-tent with your failure." View every failure as a battle, not the whole war, and each battle as an opportunity to get smarter and grow stronger.

When you're down, get up. You were created with incredible poten-tial. You are alive, and only you change your future. You are a favored child of God, and God doesn't make junk! With God's help, you will succeed and reach your dreams. In his eyes you are no loser; in fact, you're destined to win.

13

$\sim$

Turning Burnout
into Burn On

A man can no more diminish God's glory by refusing to worship
than a lunatic can put out the sun by scribbling the word
darkness on the walls of his cell.

—C. S. LEWIS

On my way to work each day, I pass a driving range. Next to the
entrance stands a large, well-lit sign advertising special events. Since I
drive by the sign every day, I usually don't pay it much attention. But
one morning it read, "Have you regripped lately?"

At first the message struck me as odd; I thought someone was asking
me about my grip on life. Eventually it dawned on me that the message
really concerned the grip on a golf club.

I like my first idea better. So let me ask you: Have you felt the need
to regrip lately? With the fast pace of postmodern life and the ever-
expanding demands on our time and talent, we all find it easy to
feel overwhelmed. And when this feeling persists over time, we call it
burnout.

ARE YOU BURNED OUT?

"Burnout" is an umbrella term covering various emotions and feelings. We often mistake it for other things such as depression, discouragement, disappointment, and chronic fatigue. To get a better understanding of burnout, let's look first at what it is not.

Burnout Is Not Depression

Everyone suffers through "down" moods. Men and women endure swings of emotional ups and downs, sometimes simply because of changes in their physical condition.

Feelings of depression can have many causes, some temporary and some more lasting. Maybe a rainy day makes you feel down. Or perhaps bad news causes you to feel melancholy just as fast as good news makes you feel euphoric. Whatever the cause, a depressed feeling is not the same thing as burnout. Depression may show up as a symptom of burnout, but it doesn't cause it. Depression may signal a bad day or reveal something more serious.

Burnout Is Not Discouragement

Everyone, at some time, goes through the tunnel of discouragement. But discouragement usually has circumstantial roots. Improve the circumstance and you feel less discouraged. Win the lottery and you can feel downright born again.

Burnout, however, doesn't change to fit the circumstances. That's why you can visit Disney World, spend sinful amounts of money on vacations and distractions, and feel no better than before you left home. Discouragement is like the waves of an ocean. With the tide up, you feel up; with the tide down, you feel down. Burnout is more like a waveless ocean; you feel flat and motionless. It resides much deeper than a surface emotion.

Burnout Is Not Disappointment

Burnout is more than feeling let down. We usually associate disappointment with a specific event or relationship. It can be as simple as going to a much-touted movie, expecting a great time, and leaving two hours later feeling cheated. It can come from a coworker who failed to lift his end of a workload. It can be as commonplace as finding out your car will not be ready when promised, or your favorite team losing a must-win game.

Feelings of depression, discouragement, and disappointment usually dissipate through good diet and improved circumstances. All of them, as devastating as they may be, arise in response to events around you; external forces generally trigger them. But burnout occurs when these three emotions turn into another, more permanent and more destructive emotion: despair.

Think of despair as the telltale emotion of burnout. The despairing individual feels helpless or hopeless or both. Despair results from a lack of meaning and perspective. If I lose a sense of meaning in my activities, then what I feel is true burnout. Burnout is a progressive and pervasive sense of despair arising from the loss of meaning and the trivialization of hope.

How does someone wind up in this condition? How does one arrive at a place of feeling too burned to care and too broke not to? How about you? Are you living the life you'd hoped and God intended? Or has burnout caught you in its net?

SYMPTOMS OF BURNOUT

Burnout generates several noticeable symptoms. Let's consider a few of them.

The Warning Sign of Chronic Fatigue

Do you feel more than normal weariness after a hard day at the office? If you're so tired the moment you get off work that you go home and lay around the house tired, go to bed tired, and get up tired, probably something more than the physical is going on.

When you suffer from burnout, you need more than a good night's rest. This kind of fatigue does not go away overnight or over the weekend. You can even go away for an extended vacation and spend thousands of dollars, yet still not feel truly rested. This type of chronic fatigue is spiritual in nature. Remember, you are not a human being in search of a spiritual experience, but a spiritual being having a human experience.

A little boy noticed that his dad brought home a big briefcase every night, crammed with a lot of work. One night he got so curious that he asked, "Daddy, why do you bring that home every night?"

"Son," the father replied, "I can't get all my work done during the day so I have to bring it home."

The little boy thought for a moment, then looked at his dad and said, "Daddy, have you ever thought about asking them to put you in a slower group?"

Wouldn't it be nice if it were that easy? But life in the real world doesn't work that way.

The Warning Sign of Emotional Exhaustion

I used to read a cartoon that featured a character perpetually followed by a cloud. Does an emotional cloud hover over you? If you live from down mood to down mood, you may suffer from emotional fatigue.

I know I'm getting emotionally exhausted when I start snapping at the people around me. When I start reacting instead of responding, I know something more is going on inside me. Given the choice, most people will respond in a kind, or at least in a tempered, manner. But when you feel emotionally wiped out, the least little thing can set you off.

Suppose you're in the checkout line at the grocery store and the person in front of you has thirteen things instead of the posted maximum of twelve. You might not say anything, but you fuss and fume all the way home and bite your wife's head off for something totally unrelated. Did you know that America actually has a growing problem with grocery store rage? Customers attack other customers in the express checkout lane. Only in America!

The Warning Sign of Aimlessness

When you feel aimless, nothing seems able to pull you out of your blue mood. You constantly ask yourself "why" questions, but find few compelling answers. "Why do I work here?" "Why am I going through these motions?" "Why do I put up with this?" If you question more than you affirm, you may be aimless. If nothing can get you excited, you may be aimless.

You pick things up, look at 'em, and put 'em down. Pick 'em up, look at 'em, put 'em down. You do this at work. You do this at home. You do this with your hobbies. You do this with your friends. You do this with everything. The things that once mattered and brought you joy and satisfaction, you now pick up and put down.

Aimlessness is more than emotional dread; it's spiritual despair. And what you dread in your emotions you despair in your heart. America's search for spirituality is actually a search for meaning. Feelings of aimlessness often accompany a sense of low self-worth. "I'm nothing to nobody." You feel more like a human doing than a human being. You feel less than important to anyone or anything. The advances in technology and the isolation of people conspire to make you feel like little more than a number.

The Warning Sign of Crisis of Meaning

My childhood family watched the *Ed Sullivan Show*, religiously, every Sunday evening. I loved the plate-spinners. They placed plates on top of sticks and twirled them endlessly—six, seven, eight, or nine at a time all spinning furiously.

Life can make you feel like a plate-spinner. We're spinning someone else's plate and begin to say, "Why is that plate up there, and why is it important for me to keep it up there? Why do I need to be doing this day after seemingly endless day?" You wake up one day and say, "You know what? This doesn't have the meaning for me it once did."

This is indeed a precarious place to be. It starts out as a feeling, then becomes a thought that you entertain. Then one day you hear yourself say, "There's got to be more than this." It's past time to regrip when you start saying these words repeatedly.

Even people in the Bible faced a crisis of meaning. Consider Moses. Listen to one of his classic prayers:

I cannot carry all these people by myself; the burden is too heavy for me. If this is how you are going to treat me, put me to death right

*now—if I have found favor in your eyes—and do not let me face my
own ruin.* (NUM. 11:14–15 NIV).

Moses had grown tired of spinning other people's plates. He tired of
the complaints and the grumbling. Could these be the same men and
women just a few months before had cried out for a leader? Moses
had reached the brink of burnout. He could no longer stand the unreasonable requests of the people. How could he feed thousands? The truth
was, he couldn't. He couldn't feed the people and satisfy their needs. But
that wasn't his real problem. His real trouble was that he had forgotten
that he shouldn't and never was intended to. It had been God's idea to
deliver the people, not Moses'. God had won their release, not Moses.

Like Moses, we burn out when we take on more responsibility than
God intended us to bear. You are to love your mate, but you can't make
him or her love you back. You are to raise your children in the nurture
and love of God, but you are not responsible for their own responses.
You are to give a quality effort at work, but you can't control corporate
cutbacks.

When we start taking on more than God intended us to bear, we
soon arrive at a place where we feel both helpless and hopeless. Despair
makes us feel beyond help and hope. And those who feel helpless and
hopeless resort to all kinds of socially destructive and self-destructive
behavior. Reinhold Niebuhr said, "Despair is the fate of the realists who
know something about sin, but nothing about redemption." There
has to be some source of good news greater than the bad news we hear
continuously.

Despair leads to self-pity and feelings of insignificance. Eugene Peterson writes in *Earth and Altar,* "Self-pity reduces the universe to a
personal wound that is displayed as proof of significance."

Burnout has become endemic in our culture. Christina Maslock, a
psychologist and an early researcher into burnout, defined the phenomenon as "a syndrome of emotional exhaustion, depersonalization, and
reduced personal accomplishment that can occur among individuals
who do people work of some kind." To be "burned out" is to feel used
up. It results in a way of thinking that leads to a self-destructive way
of acting.

If I think/believe that I am helpless and hopeless, I feel worthless. If I feel worthless, I act worthless. I then choose to act in a way that proves I am worthless. My body then takes over and feels the emotion that a worthless person should feel. This progressive, destructive pathway becomes fertile ground to addictive behavior, making the downward spiral inevitable.

UNSATISFACTORY SOURCES OF MEANING

What do you do when you don't know what to do? You do what a drowning man does when he sees something floating by—you grab it. But beware, not all good things possess the power of meaning. Let's look at some of the most popular items that cannot provide meaning.

The Trap of Positions, Possessions, and Privileges

You cannot draw meaning from things, but you can find meaning in them as long as they reflect a greater reality.

You can bring meaning to your work, for example, when you remain motivated by pleasing God. Paul said it this way: "Whatever your task, put yourselves into it, as done for the Lord and not for your masters" (Col. 3:23 NRSV). But you can never draw meaning from the work itself.

You can bring meaning to your relationships, but you cannot expect another person to validate you, at least not the way you need to be validated deep down in your heart. That would be asking from another person, what God alone can do. This is what Solomon meant when he asked, "In these few days of our empty lifetimes, who can say how one's day can best be spent? . . . For who knows the future?" (Eccl. 6:12 TLB). Only God has the power of "being" within himself. And since he alone existed before everyone and everything, he alone has the right to give to everything and everyone (which includes me and you) its value, worth, and meaning.

Now slow down and carefully consider the following statement: "God created your life meaningless." He didn't create you to be a meaningless person, but to discover your meaning more and more as you mature and grow. That's why you weren't created an adult. That's why they don't give Ph.D.'s to babies. That's why life is about experience, confusion, discovery, belief, doubt, and conviction, as opposed to cold conformity and dead orthodoxy.

Let's say I'm going to the beach on vacation and you say to me, "Dave, I know you're going to the beach. I've never been to the ocean. Could you bring the ocean back to me?" I know you're kidding, but as a joke, I take a jar and put some ocean water in it. I present it to you upon my return and say, "Here's the ocean." Now, is that the same thing? Sipping seawater from a jar is not what I call experiencing the ocean. You don't hear the waves. You can't smell the salty air. You're not savoring a sunset. You still have not experienced a day at the beach.

God intended for you to enjoy all the vistas and the opportunities of what it means to be fully and creatively alive. King David says it this way: "Lord, help me to realize how brief my time on earth will be. Help me to know that I am here for but a moment more. My life is no longer than my hand! My whole lifetime is but a moment to you. Proud man! Frail as breath! A shadow! And in all his busy rushing ends in nothing. He heaps up riches for someone else to spend. And so, Lord, my only hope is in you" (Ps. 39:4–7 TLB).

BURN ON, NOT OUT

The real trick is to burn on, not burn up or out. And it is possible. There is a way to sustain a healthy and productive lifestyle that feels fulfilling and satisfying at the same time.

The only way to regrip your life is to get a solid handle on your relationship with God and his will for you in the experiences you're having right now. You are who you are, where you are, going through what you're going through—for a reason. You are not helpless or hopeless. God is good, and he has good things in store for you.

To realize all he has promised, you must exercise your power to choose. Choose an attitude of faith and fearless wonder. Change the way you're thinking about the aimlessness of your life. You have a purpose. Pursue that purpose and succeed in that purpose. Then start acting like a person on a mission from God. To help you get started, let me suggest three ways to burn on without burning out.

Ruthlessly Eliminate Hurry

If you want to enjoy the life that God intended, you must eliminate hurry. Learn from the example of Jesus Christ. He fulfilled his earthly mission at age thirty-three when the Romans crucified him. He didn't go public with his mission until he reached age thirty. In three and a half years, he accomplished everything that he came to earth to accomplish. He kept busy, but never got in a hurry. He didn't have a car, a phone, a fax, a TV ministry, or a Web site. How did he ever make it?

In 1967, expert testimony before a committee of the United States Senate claimed that laborsaving devices and technology were about to change the way we work. Within twenty years, the experts said, people would work an average of thirty-two weeks a year and twenty-two hours a week. They would retire by the time they were forty. Because of all this time saved through technological advances, the number one challenge would be what to do with our excess time.

In 1989, just two years after the Senate prophecies were due to come true, Karen S. Peterson wrote in a *USA Today* article that a person in the nineties would need a 42-hour day to accomplish everything the experts required of a well-rounded, healthy, balanced individual. This miracle day would include 30 minutes of exercise, 45 minutes for personal grooming, 2 to 4 hours with the children and a spouse, 45 minutes to read the newspaper, 1.5 hours commuting, 7 to 10 hours working, 1 to 2 hours on housekeeping and chores, 50 minutes for sex and intimacy, plus another 15 minutes here or an hour there for such activities as cooking and eating dinner, taking care of the plants, reading a book, listening to music and sleeping.[1]

Today we suffer from what we glibly call a "time crunch." We eat fast food while we drive home from work during the "rush hour" on "expressways." We use "overnight delivery" and "rapid transit." We say we're making a "mad dash" for the mall. Even the products and services we use reference the speed of life. We send important packages by "Federal Express." We use long-distance phone service called "Sprint." We manage our finances with a computer program called "Quicken." We track appointments in a "Day Runner" and we attempt to lose weight with "Slim Fast." We live way too fast—and it's so unnecessary. God doesn't demand it, so why should we let anyone else require it of us? Matthew says of our Lord, "After he had dismissed [the people around him], he went up on a mountainside by himself to pray. When evening came, he was there alone" (Matt. 14:23 NIV). Before every major decision Jesus Christ ever made, he spent the night in prayer. In other words, he slowed down.

We damage virtually all relationships by hurry, especially our relationship with God. With all our running, we just open an ever-greater distance between where we're running to and where he's waiting for us. But God is under no moral obligation to speed up his timetable to accommodate our urgency. God tells us, "Be still before the LORD, and wait patiently for him; do not fret over those who prosper in their way, over those who carry out evil devices" (Ps. 37:7 NRSV).

Despite directives like this, life continues to accelerate. Citicorp became the number one lender in America when it cut in half the number of days it takes to approve a loan. Denny's restaurants won an explosion in business when they ran a campaign that said they would serve lunch in ten minutes, guaranteed. Servers actually brought a little timer to the table so customers could keep track of whether they received a meal in ten minutes. Domino's became the number one seller of pizzas in the United States when it guaranteed to deliver its pizzas within thirty minutes. The CEO of Domino's said, "We don't sell pizza; we sell delivery." A newspaper article told about a driver for Domino's who reported that cars actually pull off to the side of the road to let him go through, like we used to do for fire trucks. We don't even do that for ambulances anymore, but we do it for Domino's pizza drivers. Why? Because we are people in a hurry.

Jesus kept busy, but never got in a hurry. He turned aside for days of rest and nights of prayer. Busy is good; hurry is bad. The most winsome people in the world are those who make you feel that they are never in a hurry.

Ruthlessly eliminate hurry from your life, or the following poem might be your epitaph:

This is the age of the half-read page,
The quick hash and the mad dash,
The bright night with the nerves tight,

The plane hop with a brief stop,
The lamp tan and the short span,
The big shot in a good spot,
The brain strain and the heart pain,
The catnap until the spring snaps,
And the fun's done.

Cultivate a Strong, Inner Life

We ought to work at our worship and play at our work, but most of us have it backward. We play at our worship and worship our work. How many times have you heard someone say, "If I didn't have my work, I don't know what I would do"?

A couple of years ago, I took my youngest daughter, Paige, to an 'N Sync concert. Concert organizers hoarded a large group of teenage girls in a holding area. They all begged for the chance to go backstage and be onstage with 'N Sync. The officials asked the girls, "What would you do to get backstage with 'N Sync?" And to a person they all replied, "OO-oo-oo, oo-oo-oo, I'd do *anything*, anything at all, just for the chance to be onstage with 'N Sync!" And you know what? They meant literally "anything."

How sad that we tend to try to turn good things into God things. I'm not suggesting I find anything wrong with enjoying a concert or a game or any other good and fun event. But when admiration turns into adoration, we risk worshiping the wrong things. The very first commandment is, "You shall have no other gods before me" (Ex. 20:3 NIV).

I don't mean here to bash boy bands, but to acknowledge that we are made to worship something or someone. We were made for love, to first receive it and then give it away to others. Those young girls at the concert expressed the same thing their mothers and their mothers' mothers did before them. They expressed the need to feel alive and in love. All of us need to worship someone who loves us completely and is worthy of our complete devotion. We exist to stand in amazement and awe of something that blows us away. We were made to worship God. And we worship not out of dread, but delight. We worship God because he alone is worthy of our worship and adoration.

Worship is a matter of the heart, and the condition of your heart determines the strength of your inner man or woman. A heart in step with the worship of God is being both redeemed and renewed. The apostle Paul said it wonderfully well:

> For this reason I kneel before the Father, from whom his whole family in heaven and on earth derives its name. I pray that out of his glorious riches he may strengthen you with power through his Spirit in your inner being, so that Christ may dwell in your hearts through faith. And I pray that you, being rooted and established in love, may have power, together with all the saints, to grasp how wide and long and high and deep is the love of Christ, and to know this love that surpasses knowledge—that you may be filled to the measure of all the fullness of God. (EPH. 3:14–19 NIV).

The more we worship God and the more we raise his worth in our lives, the stronger we become on the inside. The bigger your God, the smaller your problems. The bigger your God, the less you fear people. Worship makes God big.

The word *worship* originally meant "heavy." Have you ever heard the phrase "Heavy, dude"? Well, God is a "heavy Dude." He's weighty—or, in other words, God is not only the real deal, he is the big deal. He alone is worthy of your worship. And worshiping him, whether in church or through the quality and love you bring to your workaday world, makes you strong and more in love with life.

Nothing will replace worship. Try as you might, nothing will fill up the hole in your soul or satisfy the hunger of your heart like God.

Elevate Significance Over Success

Over my years of speaking to large groups, I have taken several "unscientific" polls. The most common one is this: "How many of you want to be successful?" I get a unanimous response almost every time.

While we all seek success, we do not all take the time to understand it. For some, success is simply the tyranny of more. Someone asked Howard Hughes, the eccentric billionaire of a past generation, "How much is enough?" to which he announced, "Just a little more!" Toddlers would give the same answer, if they could. Have you seen the top nine laws of ownership for toddlers?

1. If I like it, it's mine.
2. If it's in my hand, it's mine.
3. If I can take it from you, it's mine.
4. If I had it just a little while ago, it's mine.
5. If I'm doing anything with it, or building something with it, all the pieces that go with it are mine.
6. If it looks like mine, it's mine.
7. If I think it's mine, it's mine.
8. If I want it, it's mine.
9. It's just plain mine.

Such a list may be okay for toddlers, but adults should know better. To help me keep significance before success, I use a little memory tool called the "IR Factor." The "I" reminds me that God sets my identity. The "R" stands for my roles. While I have only one identity, I have many roles. I'm a dad, a husband, a friend, a neighbor, a speaker, and a writer. How I perform my tasks gets measured constantly. Someone has said that the formula for success is the same as for a nervous breakdown, and the formula for a nervous breakdown is to try to please everybody. That's what happens if all you are is what you do.

My "R" factor varies, depending on which role is being measured at the time and who is doing the measurements. My wife, Paula, might rate me as her husband on a scale from 1 to 10 with a "7." My daughters, Erin, Lindsey, and Paige, might give me a "6" as a father. The people I work with might give me a "5." Whatever my "R" rating is today or tomorrow, it will never be a perfect "10."

My "I," on the other hand, is a 10. I am a son of God. I am a child of God. I am known intimately and loved completely. I can never do anything that would get God to love me more than he does right now. And, thank God, I can never do anything to get him to love me less. In him I am complete and secure. That will never change. You can't change it. My mama can't change it. Nothing I ever do or achieve will make it go up or make it go down. In God's eyes I'm a "10."

Keep your "IR" factor clear in your mind and take care not to get them confused. God counsels us to trade in our success model for a significance model. Don't get me wrong; I want to be successful. I read books on success. But I understand that my success comes out of my significance. That's what the apostle John meant when he warned, "The world and its desires pass away, but the man who does the will of God lives forever" (1 John 2:17 NIV). And Jesus taught, "What's the use of worrying? What good does it do? Will it add a single day to your life? Of course not! And if worry can't even do such little things as that, what's the use of worrying over bigger things? Look at the lilies! They don't toil and spin, and yet Solomon in all his glory was not robed as well as they are. And if God provides clothing for the flowers that are here today and gone tomorrow, don't you suppose that he will provide clothing for you, you doubters? And don't worry about food—what to eat and drink; don't worry at all that God will provide it for you. All mankind scratches for its daily bread, but your heavenly Father knows your needs" (Luke 12:25–30 TLB).

Amy Saltzman, associate editor for *U.S. News and World Report*, wrote a book titled *Downshifting: Reinventing Success on a Slower Track*. She suggests a shift from the idea that success means more things and more responsibility with less time to enjoy either, to a paradigm that values better relationships and more time to enjoy them.

Success is not more stuff, but a closer walk with Christ and more loving relationships with God's children. In her first chapter, "The Solitude of Empty Porches," Saltzman talks about walking down Newark Street in Washington, D.C. Living in one of the old Victorian homes on Newark Street has become a status symbol for Washington, D.C., professionals. Saltzman says that the "gracious romantic porches are tailor-made for reading Faulkner, chatting with the neighbors, watching the world go by. . . . It is a realtor's dream, with homes that typically sell for upwards of $1 million." But the porches remain empty. "In all the times I [have] walked down Newark Street," she writes, "I [have] never once seen anyone sitting on even one of those picture-perfect porches." The image of those "beautiful, empty million-dollar facades . . . in one neat snapshot . . . said it all." And how does she describe those who live alone inside those homes? She sees "emptiness in the midst of luxury, wealth in the midst of despair."[2]

So which do you choose? Success or significance? Despair or joy? It's really up to you.

RECEIVE GOD'S BLESSINGS

Saint Augustine said, "God is more anxious to bestow his blessings on us than we are to receive them." So if God is willing and you are ready, remember that burnout is more than depression, discouragement, and disappointment. It is a loss of meaning that leads only to one place: despair. And despair leads to feeling helpless and hopeless.

Burnout's symptoms include chronic fatigue, emotional exhaustion, and aimlessness, which lead to a crisis of meaning. You restore meaning and direction in your life by ruthlessly eliminating hurry, cultivating a strong inner life, and elevating significance over success.

The power to prevail provides the tools and the motivation to burn on, not out. Yes, the road is long and the way fraught with danger. But God feels neither tired nor worried. Let him carry you through to ultimate victory!

14

Turning Regret into Resolve

Regret is an appalling waste of energy; you can't build on it; it's good only for wallowing in.

–KATHERINE MANSFIELD

On his first day on the job, a young assistant football coach found himself on his first crucial recruiting trip. He wanted to do well, so he asked the head coach to give him a clear vision regarding the type of player the team needed.

"You've seen players who stay down after they get hit?" asked the head coach.

"Yes," the rookie said with a nod. "I know we don't want any of those guys!"

"Right," said the head coach, then he added, "You've also seen those guys who get hit again and again by a big fullback and they get knocked flat on their backs and bounce right back up for more?"

"Yeah, I've gotcha, Coach!" replied the new assistant. "You want me to go out and get those for you, right?"

"Nah," growled the old veteran. "I want you to go and get me that fullback!"

Life is about forward motion, and if you wait to be acted upon, you're likely to lose. In tennis, it's called serve and volley; in football it's called offense vs. defense. In life it's living as though right now counts forever. Because it does.

THE HABIT OF REGRET

Regret tries to move forward while looking backward. Resolve lives offensively with a view toward the future.

Forward motion and focus require that we stop talking about the past and start talking about our plans for the future. Let's stop worrying about things that can't be changed. There is no power in the things you didn't do but you should have done, or the things that you did that you shouldn't have done. Dwelling on them robs you of the present and the future.

If you need forgiveness for what you've done or failed to do, then confess it to God. Claim this promise: "If we confess our sins, he who is faithful and just will forgive us our sins and cleanse us from all unrighteousness" (1 John 1:9 NRSV). If you've confessed the sins of the past, then rejoice in another promise: "Oh, what joy for those whose rebellion is forgiven, whose sin is put out of sight!" (Ps. 32:1 NLT).

If you haven't experienced God's forgiving power, stop now and ask for it. Maybe you've asked God to forgive you, but you continue to ask him to forgive things for which you've already received forgiveness. I wonder if God sometimes says, "If you'll quit bringing it up, so will I." To get stuck in guilt is to be gripped by the habits of regret. Regret thrives on three self-defeating habits: placing blame, shaming myself, and defaming others.

Blaming Leaves Me a Victim

Blame is all about shifting responsibility. When we live with regret, we want someone to blame. It doesn't matter if the person, place, or thing has no relation to where we are today. As long as we can point the finger at someone or something and pronounce them guilty of whatever happened, we get some temporary relief.

But placing blame is equally about playing the role of victim. Once we adopt the identity of a victim, we find it hard to hold out any hope for the future. Blaming originates in an attitude of entitlement, an attitude that never feels satisfied because it never believes it has all it rightly deserves.

Shaming Leaves Me Helpless

I remember taking my report card home and hearing my mother say, "You ought to be ashamed of yourself." I wanted to say, "Thanks, but I don't need any help from you to feel really, really bad."

The shaming didn't end with my report cards. It carried over to my relationships. But I don't need help from outsiders on the shaming deal; I'm there all by myself. From as far back as I can remember, I have collected these shaming tapes in my head. And anytime or at anyplace when I mess up, a shaming memory confirms that I'm stupid, inept, and inferior.

If you take those early shame tapes that you received from your parents, siblings, teachers, preachers, or coaches, and play them over and over, you can't help but end up feeling helpless. Shame is both toxic and debilitating.

Defaming Others Shifts Responsibility

When we defame others, we try to shift the shame from ourselves to someone else. We project onto another the behavior we find abhorrent in ourselves.

A "Peanuts" cartoon showed Peppermint Patty talking to Charlie Brown. "Guess what, Chuck," she said. "The first day of school, and I got sent to the principal's office. It was your fault, Chuck."

"My fault?" he sputtered. "How could it be my fault? Why do you say everything is my fault?"

"You're my friend, aren't you, Chuck?"

"Yes, of course."

"You should've been a better influence on me."

Like Peppermint Patty, some people actually think someone else is responsible for their choices.

HOW TO AVOID REGRET

Would you like to tame your regrets? Then stop the behavior that creates them. Consider three temptations that you will never regret avoiding.

The Shortcuts You Didn't Take

In life, there are no shortcuts to anyplace worth going. There are no shortcuts to the good life God has planned for you. You cannot get ahead by being dishonest. God keeps score.

Don't give in to the temptation. Don't listen to the allure of quick profit, fast promotion, or overnight success. I once asked someone dubbed an overnight success how he did it. "It's easy," he replied. "Just give twenty-five years of sweat, suffering, and sacrifice, and you, too, can be an 'overnight success.'"

If you're in a hurry, don't be. Don't let your impatience to "get on with life" lead you down the wrong road. Jesus gave a stern warning to those looking for a short walk around the extra mile: "Enter through the narrow gate. For wide is the gate and broad is the road that leads to destruction, and many enter through it. But small is the gate and narrow the road that leads to life, and only a few find it" (Matt. 7:13–14 NIV).

The Unholy Itch You Didn't Scratch

We tend to underestimate how much pressure we can stand, and overestimate how much temptation we can endure. Don't get those two things mixed up. Everyone has an unholy itch they're tempted to scratch. Don't do it! It's not worth it.

A young guy named Mark was a better-than-average student at everything but spelling. During one particularly difficult spelling test, he felt stumped by many difficult words. Softly the tempter whispered,

"Look at Jane's paper; she's an honor student and always gets them right!" Mark heeded the suggestion and copied several answers. The teacher noticed his actions and felt great surprise, for she had always thought of him as an honest kid.

When it came time to collect the work, she observed an internal struggle in Mark. After bowing his head for a moment, he suddenly tore up his paper. Although at first he had yielded to temptation, he finally decided to take a zero rather than be dishonest.

Calling the boy to her desk, the teacher said, "I was watching you, Mark, and I want you to know that I'm very proud of you for what you did just now. Today you really passed a much greater examination than your spelling test!"

A Greek proverb says, "One minute of patience, ten years of peace." You will never regret not giving in to temptation.

Refusing to Get Even

Someone will treat you unfairly. Accept it. Any time spent plotting your revenge is too much. As the old saying goes, "You can chase down a skunk and catch it, but is it really worth it?"

In his book *None of These Diseases,* Dr. S. I. McMillen says, "It might be written on many thousands of death certificates that the victim died of grudge-itis. Grudge-itis is responsible for such things as ulcers, high blood pressure, and strokes. The moment I start hating a man, I become his slave."

I can't enjoy my work if someone else dominates my thoughts. Strong feelings of resentment produce too many stress hormones. I become fatigued after only a few hours of work. The man I hate may live miles from my bedroom, but more cruel than any slave driver, he whips my thoughts into such a frenzy that my innerspring mattress becomes a rack of torture. I become the slave of anyone with whom I feel I must get even.

Is getting even important to you? Then make a habit of getting even with those who have helped you, not those you think wronged you. Be the fullback who delivers the hit in an attempt to get the ball down the field, rather than the linebacker who accepts the hits. Energy spent in getting even is always better spent getting ahead. The past is for reflection, the present for rejoicing, and the future for resolving. And a person with resolve has the power to prevail. She transforms regrets into forward motion.

Once you make your decisions, your decisions make you. Make the firm determination right now to be the fullback.

TURNING REGRET INTO RESOLVE

Not long ago I audited a doctoral seminar on leadership. One day the professor asked each of the sixteen participants in his class to tell the one thing at which they excelled. I dread questions like these, because I still am not sure of what I do best; and besides, it sounds like bragging.

When my turn came, all I could think to say was, "I am best at not quitting." That sounded a little strange at first, but the more I think about it, the happier I am with my answer. At first it didn't sound like much of a skill, but when you consider all the adversities we face, the power to prevail becomes priceless. When you're going through hell on earth, the ability not to stop and smell the smoke can make the difference between success and failure, between significance and scandal.

Albert Einstein said, "It's not that I'm so smart, it's just that I stay with problems longer." Einstein dramatically illustrates the power to prevail. Powerful is the man or woman who knows how to find advantage in adversity and who uses it to prevail against all odds!

I find it easier to prevail when I use a list of resolutions I made for myself. They help me to recalibrate when I get distracted. Maybe they will help you, too.

I Resolve to Be Real

The world brims over with posers and phonies. Too many people pretend to be what they're not. Why? The world tells us to put on a mask and cover up. God wants us to get out from behind the mask and get real.

Remember, whatever we uncover and confess to God, he will cover and convert. The process makes us transparent and real.

I believe in a God who loves me like I am but who loves me too much to leave me where I am. The Scripture admonishes us, "Never pay back evil for evil. Do things in such a way that everyone can see you are honest clear through" (Rom. 12:17 TLB). Since I resolve to be real, my life will gravitate toward love, not lust; joy, not jealousy; gladness, not grief; faith, not fear; dreams, not dreads; and burn on, not burn out!

I Resolve to Be Right

Pascal, the French mathematician and philosopher, once wrote, "Knowing God without knowing our wretchedness leads to pride. Knowing our wretchedness without knowing God leads to despair."

I do not want to stand before God on the grounds of my good intentions. I want to find out what is right and live by it. Jesus said, "I am the way and the truth and the life. No one comes to the Father except through me" (John 14:6 NIV). Christianity is the only world religion that says we do not have the right to force anyone to conform to our beliefs. If we can't win your heart, we will not use our hand to make you comply.

All of life ought to be a search for the truth. Jesus told those who believed in him, "If you hold to my teaching, you are really my disciples. Then you will know the truth, and the truth will set you free" (John 8:31–32 NIV). I love that staggering promise of freedom!

I resolve to follow the Christ who came to destroy race barriers and class hatred. I resolve to love and obey the only Savior in whom all races have their ideal. His cross bridges every chasm. His love overcomes hate. His joy outshines any happiness. He gave womanhood its place, childhood its rights, and the slave his freedom. When I follow him wholeheartedly, I never feel confused or afraid!

I Resolve to Be Redemptive

To be a follower of Christ is to be redemptive. That means that our mission in life is to be a part of a global effort to right what is wrong, to bring people together, and to knock down artificial barriers.

In Christ there is no black, white, purple, green, or polka-dot. In

Christianity, Democrat or Republican, good or bad, rich or poor, all can go to heaven, because Christ alone has paid the price of our redemption. And to be like him is to spread the good news of God's call to whosoever will come and drink of the water of life freely.

I love being a Christian because my job is simply to find a way to help bring people together, to help people find love, to help them get to God, and to help them come to a place where they can let God love them. Unlike religion, which is about rules, Christianity is about a relationship. God wants to include as many people as possible in his kingdom. Religion excludes and seeks to separate people. Christianity seeks to save and include. Jesus said it this way: "For the Son of Man came to seek and save what was lost" (Luke 19:10 NIV).

I Resolve to Be Enthusiastic

If you have no other talent, just showing up and smiling will go a long way. I feel amazed at those who, despite their rich blessings, unique gifts, and extensive education, look like they're bored to death. If you're going to act dead, then fall over! But if you're going to live, then act like it. Stand tall, shoulders square, chin up, and choose to be grateful. Get excited about every day. Cherish every moment as a gift from God.

It doesn't matter how you express your enthusiasm; just do it! Want a good place to start showing your joy? Then try it at work. Listen to this command from Scripture: "Never be lazy in your work, but serve the Lord enthusiastically" (Rom. 12:11 TLB). Resolve to be enthusiastic and you will bring your own party atmosphere to work. Mother Teresa put it this way: "It does not matter what you do. It matters only how much love you put into what you do."

Maybe you're not working at your dream job. Maybe you don't work around people whom you like. If you don't like your coworkers, then get another job and God will take those people with you. Listen to the proper perspective: "Whatever you do, work at it with all your heart, as working for the Lord, not for men" (Col. 3:23 NIV).

I resolve to be enthusiastic in my work world because I know that I work for the Lord. And if I work for the Lord, then I can expect my reward to come from the Lord.

I Resolve to Be Positive

A positive person sees life through a faith filter. You can recognize such individuals by the questions they ask. They like "what" and "why" questions—queries about purpose and passion. Positive people know what they're doing and why they're doing it. They have a big-picture mentality and an "act small" ability. Circumstances and trends do not sway or sour their outlook. They consider their mission important and know they will prevail if they keep their eyes on the prize.

By contrast, a negative person looks at life through a lens of fear. You can recognize these folks by their obsessive preoccupation with "How?" questions. They wonder how any new proposal could ever work, given the current lack of resources. Negative people focus on problems and prohibitions. They don't want to use their imagination or creativity capabilities, so their hope atrophies. And as hope shrinks, the seeds of faith cannot penetrate the hardened soil.

I know men who will remain single for the rest of their lives because they're scared. "If I marry her," they say, "how do I know that we'll stay together?" Answer: you don't! Take some chances. Dare to risk something. Squeeze the toothpaste from the middle from time to time and see what happens. Rip the tags off the mattress and see if the police show up!

I have learned that a big "why" will attract its own "how." If you start with "how," you will paralyze yourself into inactivity. I discovered this firsthand when my wife and I dared to plant a brand-new church. When we shared our dream of a church plant without buildings, budgets, or backing, all most people could ask was, "How are you going to do it?"

"I don't know!" I replied.

"How are you going to gather a committed core?"

"I don't know!"

"How will you find a meeting place?"

"I don't know!"

When we started meeting in a school, the question became, "How are we going to have our own facility?"

I could only reply, "I don't know right now, and I don't need to know that 'how' right now."

Today, the church my wife and I planted sits on 280 acres, on a major interstate in our city. How it happened is a miracle and a confirmation that we set out on a legitimate venture.

I Resolve to Be Virtuous

I want to be a man of honor. I want to be known as a lover of God and a builder of people. Every day I pray, "Dear God, make me a man of God."

An old hymn expresses my prayer: "I want to be a man after God's own heart." That's what I want. I want to be "after" God's heart in the sense that I love him and long to be more like what he had in mind when he created me. I also want to be a man "after" God's own heart in that I reflect his love in the ways I conduct my life. I long to be honest, not merely because honesty is the best policy, but because honest is what God is.

Listen to Jesus' words: "In the same way, let your light shine before men, that they may see your good deeds and praise your Father in heaven" (Matt. 5:16 NIV). God intends that people look at our lives, see the virtue in them, and feel attracted to the virtue they see.

I Resolve to Be Dangerous

There is still a little of the rebel left in me. I want to be good, but not boring. I want to be virtuous *and* dangerous.

I don't want to be Mister Rogers nice. I want to be William Wallace brave. I want to do something significant with my life. I want to change something. I want an adventure. I want to win a war, right a wrong, and rescue a damsel in distress. I think that's what every man wants.

John Eldredge, in his great book *Wild at Heart,* expresses the same resolve when he suggests, "In the heart of every man is the desire for a battle to fight, an adventure to live, and a beauty to rescue."[1]

I long to be dangerous and at the same time virtuous. The combination of danger and virtue defines nobility—braveheartedness. How many times does the Bible tell us, "Be of good courage"? Fear not! Be bold, for the Lord thy God is with thee. Listen to Jesus' words: "I am sending you out like sheep among wolves. Therefore be as shrewd as snakes and as innocent as doves" (Matt. 10:16 NIV). God's way is to be smart and strong, sensitive and careful.

With God's help, I will stir up the status quo, strive for excellence, and stand for righteousness until the day I die. I will comfort the afflicted and afflict the comfortable. I will push people out of their corners and comfort zones and into the public arena of ideas. I will dare to attempt great things. I will dare to attempt something so big, so bold, and so life-changing that I'm doomed for failure if God doesn't show up.

I Resolve to Be a Builder

The majority of people I meet fall into one of three categories: the broken, the bruised, or the bored.

The broken have seen their hopes crumble under the rocks of reality. Someone has broken a promise, betrayed them, or cheated them, and they feel broken by the unrelenting harshness of life. They actually feel "broken" inside.

The bruised doubt things will ever turn out for them the way they had imagined. They feel disappointed with life and with God. They feel put out and put upon by the insensitivity of people and the unresponsiveness of God.

The bored have seemingly led a charmed life. Everything they touch turns to gold. They are the envy of their friends and a great source of aggravation to their foes. They have it all. And therein lies the rub. They suffer from success sickness. When they survey their lives, they ask, "Is this all there is?"

This is where the gospel of Christ comes in. God directs the good news of his grace to the broken, the bruised, and the bored. According to the gospel, no one is so broke that God can't heal them, no one so bruised that God can't comfort them, and no one so bored that God can't wake them up.

I have resolved to build up people in their relationship with God. That is why, at the tender age of eighteen, I decided to spend my life trying to strengthen others through the vehicle that Christ ordained, the church. Jesus said, "I will build my church, and the gates of Hades

will not overcome it" (Matt. 16:18 NIV). The church that Jesus envi-
sioned is made up not of brick and mortar, but of people. And while
buildings are great tools, they don't begin to compare to the trophies of
God's grace—the sweet, amazing people who have tuned in to God's
love, tanked up on God's grace, and turned out into the world to build
up others by holding out hope.

I resolve to spend my life building up men and women, boys and
girls—not on an assembly line, but as a farmer who plants a healthy
crop. I plant the good seed, and God gives a great harvest. The apostle
Paul set the standard for the priority of building up people. "By the
grace God has given me," he wrote, "I laid a foundation as an expert
builder, and someone else is building on it. But each one should be careful how he builds. For no one can lay any foundation other than the one
already laid, which is Jesus Christ. If any man builds on this foundation
using gold, silver, costly stones, wood, hay or straw, his work will be
shown for what it is, because the Day will bring it to light. It will
be revealed with fire, and the fire will test the quality of each man's
work. If what he has built survives, he will receive his reward" (1 Cor.
3:10–14 NIV).

I Resolve to Do My Best

I long to be the best me that God created me to be. God has given all
of us great potential. To God, you are not one in a million; you're one in
six billion. No one has ever been born with your fingerprint or DNA.
You are where you are and who you are by the will of God. So spend the
rest of your life living up to it!

I resolve, in God's name, to do my best. I'm not going to fight my
battles with your armor. I'm going to live my life before God as an audience of one.

If you try to do anyone else's best, you will grow miserable. You cannot please people, so don't even try. You can love 'em, you can provide
for 'em, and you can even take a bullet for 'em—but you can't make
them happy. At the end of your life you want to hear, "Well done, thou
good and faithful servant. . . . Enter thou into the joy of thy lord"
(Matt. 25:21 KJV).

I Resolve to Enjoy the Journey

Frederick Buechner, in his great little book *The Last Analysis,* says, "All moments are key moments and life itself is grace. Every moment, the big, obviously dramatic ones, and the real small, apparently insignificant ones, every moment is key. Every one is precious. Every one is God's gift to you, and you must learn to live in it."

Through sickness, we recognize the value of health; through evil, the value of virtue; through hunger, the value of food; through work, the value of rest.

I Resolve to Prevail

With God's help and by his grace, I will prevail. I don't intend merely to survive, but to thrive. Those who prevail face the worst that life can throw at them while they stand strong, defiant in the face of forces that would bury them and reliant on the God who seeks to build them up.

I think of the farmer whose mule had fallen into an old, dry well. He loved this mule; the beast had been with him so long. He got all his buddies together and asked, "How are we going to get this mule out of here?" The group agreed that he might as well shoot the mule, because he'd kill it trying to bring it up. So he got his shotgun, loaded it, aimed it, and just before he squeezed the trigger, the mule gazed up at him with a look that said, "I'm your friend. How could you shoot me after all we've been through?"

The farmer couldn't bring himself to shoot the mule. So he came up with the idea to bury the mule alive. As he shoveled the dirt, big clouds of dust billowed up. Every time he got a load of dirt on the back of that mule, the beast would shake it off and step up. The farmer kept it up until his mule walked right out of the dry well.

If you are to prevail, you must learn a lesson from the mule. A whole lot of people are going to put dirt on your back. If you spend your life craning your neck to see who's doing it, you'll get buried alive. Shake off that dirt and step up. Live out the old Japanese proverb: "Fall seven times; stand up eight."

The power to prevail gives you the ability to move ahead in victory because retreat is not an option. When Hernán Cortés landed on the shores of Mexico with a small but well-equipped army, he made a daring move to guarantee the success of his campaign. He set ablaze the only ships that could take his soldiers back to Spain. By this act of total resolve, Cortés eliminated the possibility of a pullback. Now that his troops had no way to return home, they had nothing left to do but commit fully to final victory. And that is precisely what they did.

I Resolve to Finish Well

In *Alice in Wonderland,* the king says to the White Rabbit, "Begin at the beginning and go on till you come to the end; then stop."

Humorist Erma Bombeck said, "When I stand before God at the end of my life, I would hope that I would not have a single bit of talent left, and could say: I used everything you gave me."

Thomas Paine put it this way: "'Tis the business of little minds to shrink, but he whose heart is firm, and whose conscience approves his conduct, will pursue his principles unto death."

J. P. Morgan, commenting on the life of Napoleon Bonaparte, said, "No obstacles fell in his way that seemed to him insurmountable. He might be defeated, as he sometimes was, but he shrank from no hardship through impatience, he fled from no danger through cowardice."

BREAK THE TAPE

I pray that God would give you the power to prevail, like a champion runner stretching with every ounce of strength to break the tape at the finish line. I pray that you would take the ideas in this book and the truth of God's love and with strength and purpose hit the line of adversity and regret . . . and come away a winner.

I leave you with some wise words from the poem "The Quitter," by Canadian poet Robert Service:

It's easy to cry that you're beaten—and die;
It's easy to crawfish and crawl;
But to fight and to fight when hope's out of sight—
Why, that's the best game of them all!
And though you come out of each grueling bout,
All broken and beaten and scarred,
Just have one more try—it's dead easy to die,
It's the keeping-on-living that's hard.

To learn more about the author and his ministry
and the ideas expressed in *The Power to Prevail*,
visit his website at

http://www.fosteringhope.com

Notes

Chapter 1

1. Stuart Briscoe, *Bound for Joy* (Ventura, CA: Regal Books, 1984), 95.
2. Paul Stoltz, *Adversity Quotient* (New York: John Wiley & Sons, Inc., 1997), 5.
3. Jim Collins, *Good to Great* (New York: Harper, 2001), 42.

Chapter 2

1. Gerald Mann, *When the Bad Times Are Over for Good* (Austin, TX: Riverbend Press, 1992), 151.

Chapter 3

1. Jerry Potter, "Last Call for Palmer at Augusta," *USA Today;* 4-14-02.

Chapter 4

1. C. S. Lewis, *Surprised by Joy* (Eugene, OR: Harvest House, 1975).
2. C. S. Lewis, *Mere Christianity* (New York: HarperCollins, 1952), 50.
3. Paul Tillich, *The New Being* (New York: Charles Scribner, 1955).
4. Clyde Reid, *Celebrate the Temporary* (San Francisco, CA: Harper, 1974), 44–45.
5. Associated Press, March 2, 2001.

Chapter 5

1. Lisa Beamer with Ken Abraham, *Let's Roll* (Wheaton, IL: Tyndale House, 2002), 307–8.

Chapter 6

1. William James, *Energies of Men* (Kila, MT: Kessinger Publishing, 1998).

Chapter 8

1. London Reuters, February 22, 2002.

Chapter 11

1. Mike Littwin, "Name That 'Toon: This Warner Brother Production Almost Too Good to Be Believed," *Denver Rocky Mountain News*, January 26, 2000, final edition.
2. Dave and Jan Dravecky, *When You Can't Come Back* (New York: Harper-Collins, 1992).
3. *20/20*, ABC-TV, May 25, 1993.

Chapter 13

1. Karen S. Peterson, "There's No Way to Beat the Clock!" *USA Today*, April 13, 1989.
2. Amy Saltzman, *Downshifting: Reinventing Success on a Slower Track* (New York: HarperCollins, 1991), 13–15.

Chapter 14

1. John Eldredge, *Wild at Heart* (Nashville: Thomas Nelson, 2001), 9.